INSTITUTE OF LEADERSHIP & MANAGEMENT

SUPERSERIES

Solving
Problems

FOURTH EDITION

Published for the
Institute of Leadership & Management by **Pergamon Flexible Learning**

AMSTERDAM • BOSTON • HEIDELBERG • LONDON • NEW YORK • OXFORD
PARIS • SAN DIEGO • SAN FRANCISCO • SINGAPORE • SYDNEY • TOKYO

Pergamon Flexible Learning
An imprint of Elsevier
Linacre House, Jordan Hill, Oxford OX2 8DP
30 Corporate Drive, Burlington, MA 01803

First published 1986
Second edition 1991
Third edition 1997
Fourth edition 2003
Reprinted 2004 (twice)

British Library Cataloguing in Publication Data
A catalogue record for this book is available from the British Library

ISBN 0 7506 5818 5

For information on Pergamon Flexible Learning
visit our website at www.bh.com/pergamonfl

Institute of Leadership & Management
registered office
1 Giltspur Street
London
EC1A 9DD
Telephone 020 7294 3053
www.i-l-m.com
ILM is a subsidiary of the City & Guilds Group

The views expressed in this work are those of the authors and do
not necessarily reflect those of the Institute of Leadership and
Management or of the publisher

Author: Howard Senter
Editor: Dela Jenkins
Editorial management: Genesys, www.genesys-consultants.com
Based on previous material by: Joe Johnson
Composition by Genesis Typesetting, Rochester, Kent
Printed and bound in Great Britain by MPG Books, Bodmin

Contents

Contents

Workbook introduction

1 ILM Super Series study links

This workbook addresses the issues of *Solving Problems*. Should you wish to extend your study to other Super Series workbooks covering related or different subject areas, you will find a comprehensive list at the back of this book.

2 Links to ILM Qualifications

This workbook relates to the following learning outcomes in segments from the ILM Level 3 Introductory Certificate in First Line Management and the Level 3 Certificate.

    C2.2   Problem solving skills
        1 Recognise existence, nature and scope of problem
        2 Identify relevant objectives
        3 Identify options for resolving the problem
        4 Evaluate effectiveness of options
        5 Recommend optimum solution within circumstances
        6 Monitor and review chosen solution to ensure objectives achieved

3 Links to S/NVQs in Management

This workbook relates to the following elements of the Management Standards which are used in S/NVQs in Management, as well as a range of other S/NVQs.

A1.3   Make recommendations for improvements to work activities
C1.1   Develop your own skills to improve your performance
D1.1   Gather required information
D1.2   Inform and advise others.

It will also help you develop the following Personal Competences:

- focusing on results;
- searching for information;
- thinking and taking decisions.

4 Workbook objectives

We all encounter problems in every sphere of our lives, but in a management context they are particularly important. In fact, it's often claimed that the most important things that managers have to do are to solve problems and make decisions.

Problem-solving and decision-making are closely connected. Choosing a solution, for example (the subject of Session C in this workbook), is basically about **deciding** which possible solution to adopt.

Nevertheless, there is a distinction between problem-solving and decision-making. Managers, supervisors and team leaders become aware of it when they investigate and report a problem – but have to pass it up the line for a decision. Decisions are often made by a higher level of management, after a searching analysis of the costs, benefits and risks of each decision option.

Problem-solving and decision-making can be seen as two ends of the same process. This workbook is only concerned with the problem-solving end of things. Consequently, the focus is primarily on identifying and understanding problems and seeking possible causes. The decision-making end of things is greatly simplified.

Some problems are quite easy to deal with but, unfortunately, a lot of the problems that you and other managers, supervisors and team leaders will face are anything but clear-cut. Often you will find that in addition to being difficult to solve:

- problems are hard to pin down and describe clearly
- the causes are obscure
- there are several possible solutions, and it's unclear which would be best
- the best solutions seem difficult to put into effect.

Fortunately, if we adopt a careful and systematic approach, there are few problems that cannot be tackled successfully. In the four workbook sessions that follow you will be taken through a six-stage process for solving problems:

- **recognize** the problem
- accept **ownership** of the problem
- **understand** the problem
- **choose** the best solution
- **implement** the solution
- monitor and **evaluate** the solution.

We will consider how to decide whether problems are our responsibility, and whether they are worth spending time and energy on. We will look at ways of describing and dissecting problems, so that their causes can be pinned down accurately. There will be coverage of practical techniques like brainstorming and problem analysis, and of some approaches to matching causes and solutions. Finally, the most important, but perhaps least exciting stage of the process will be addressed – ensuring that your solutions work in practice.

4.1 Objectives

When you have completed this workbook you will be better able to:

- describe and analyse problems;
- identify the cause or causes of problems;
- generate a range of possible solutions and decide which will work best;
- implement your chosen solutions and evaluate their effectiveness.

5 Activity planner

You may want to look at the following Activities now, so that you can start collecting material – or do whatever else is required – as soon as possible:

Activity 4 on pages 4–5 asks you to review some problems that you have recently had to deal with. The main aim here is to identify problems that were not foreseen, but could have been, and to understand why this was.

Activity 8 on page 12 is the first in a series of eight activities in which you will be asked to analyse a problem that is facing you at work.

Activity 18 on page 29 is designed to give you practice in brainstorming, a key technique in management. You will need to get together with some friends or colleagues in order to do this.

Activity 23 on page 38 asks you to compile a list of people whose skills and experience might be of use to you when setting out to solve a problem at work.

Some or all of these Activities may provide the basis of evidence for your S/NVQ portfolio. All Portfolio Activities and the Work-based assignment are signposted with this icon.

The icon states the elements to which the Portfolio Activities and Work-based assignment relate.

If you are compiling an S/NVQ portfolio, you may like to develop further Activities 4, 8, 13, 15, 23, 25, 33, 35 and 42 and the Work-based assignment as evidence of your competence. They are all marked with the portfolio icon shown on the left.

Session A
Problems large and small

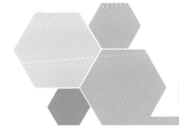

1 Introduction

Problems come in all forms, shapes and sizes. The problem in Activity 1 appears to be a simple one.

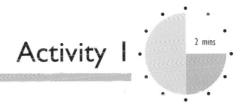

Activity 1 · 2 mins

What would you do if you were offered the choice of:

a   receiving £1 million in one lump sum;

b   getting just one penny on the first day of a month, two on the second day, four on the third, eight pennies on the fourth and so on, to the end of the month?

It may look like a simple choice, but you would be well advised to sit down with pencil and paper and/or calculator, and work out which option is better. You will find the answer on page 96.

This little puzzle illustrates the theme of the first part of the workbook.

It's a good idea to think about the problem before coming up with a solution!

2 What do we mean by 'a problem'?

'Problem' is one of those words we use loosely to describe any situation which looks uncertain or difficult in any respect. For the purposes of this workbook we need to be more specific about what we mean.

Activity 2

3 mins

Write down in your own words a definition of the word 'problem'.

_____

_____

You might have answered:

- something hard to understand;
- a doubtful or difficult question;
- something difficult to control, which disrupts smooth progress;
- a puzzle or mystery of some kind;
- a task that is difficult to carry out.

All of these would be correct, but the definition on which this workbook is based is:

Something which is difficult to deal with or to resolve.

Of course, some problems are more difficult to deal with than others.

In this workbook we will be concerned with those problems which appear to offer no easy solution; especially the kind that makes us feel we don't know where to begin.

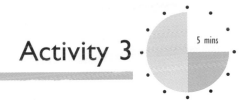

Activity 3 · 5 mins

Think about some problems you've had at work recently. Try to make a list of at least three different **kinds** of problem. You don't need to worry about the details at this stage; just make a note of the general type of problem you seemed to be dealing with (for example, relations between members of the workteam).

_____

_____

_____

The list of possible problems at work could be endless; the following are just some suggestions to which many more could be added.

■ **Deviation problems:** where something has gone wrong, and **corrective action is needed**. For example:

- ■ equipment malfunction;
- ■ supplies not received;
- ■ illness among the workteam;
- ■ 'log jams' of work or people.

■ **Potential problems:** where problems may be arising for the future and **preventive** action is needed. For example:

- ■ strong rivalries between members of the workteam;
- ■ increased demand which you may have difficulty meeting;
- ■ growing staff turnover.

■ **improvement problems:** how to be more productive, efficient and responsive in the future. For example:

- ■ upgrading products, premises, equipment or methods;
- ■ installing a new system;
- ■ equipping people with new skills;
- ■ changing procedures to meet new safety standards.

In this workbook we will look at techniques which you can apply to problems in all sorts of situations.

The first of these techniques, and perhaps the most important of all, is really about an **attitude of mind**. Perhaps you've heard the expression: 'When you are up to your knees in alligators, it's difficult to remember that it's your job to clear the swamp.'

Detach yourself from the problem. Be objective. Analyse. Stand clear of the alligators!

You probably feel that you are 'up to your knees in alligators' much of the time. It may be as much as you can do to stop yourself being eaten alive by the problems that surround you, let alone solve them. The only thing to do is to 'get out of the swamp'.

3 Problems foreseen and unforeseen

'Problems, like accidents, can always be prevented.'

Do you agree with this statement? Or do you believe that, as an individual, you can't always prevent or foresee what happens to you? Perhaps you feel that there are cases where **you** can see problems arising, but you can't convince others that they should be taken seriously?

> While her boss was away, someone asked Ruth, the senior technician, whether the new computers had been ordered. She knew they hadn't, but since her boss had obtained several quotations, she identified the cheapest that met the specification, and placed the order. Of the 11 computers delivered, all but two had faults in the operating software, which, it soon emerged, had been copied illegally by what was in fact a 'rogue' supplier. It didn't occur to Ruth to consider which suppliers were reliable and which weren't. But if her boss had been there, this problem probably wouldn't have arisen.

Activity 4

15 mins

S/NVQ A1.3

This Activity may provide the basis of appropriate evidence for your S/NVQ portfolio. If you are intending to take this course of action, it might be better to write your answers on separate sheets of paper.

Think about some problems involving your work that have arisen in recent weeks or months.

Try to identify four altogether: two which you **could not** have foreseen or prevented, and two which you feel **could have** been foreseen and prevented, but which weren't. Write brief details below.

Could not have foreseen or prevented:

1 _____

_____

_____

2 _____

_____

_____

Could have foreseen and prevented:

1 _____

_____

_____

2 _____

_____

_____

Now think again about these problems.

Are you **sure** that the 'unforeseeable' ones really couldn't have been anticipated?

Why was it that the 'foreseeable' ones **weren't** anticipated?

What lessons can you draw from this? What will you personally do differently in future?

Being able to anticipate and prevent problems is a basic management skill, so you should try to learn lessons from situations like these. From now on, as you encounter situations which may turn out to be problems, try to 'get your retaliation in early'.

You probably thought of several situations where a little more planning and forethought would have prevented a problem from developing. You should always try to ensure that a problem doesn't occur in the first place. Failing this, bear in mind that the chosen solution to a problem should always include plans to prevent the problem happening again.

4 The six stages of problem-solving

There are six stages to the problem-solving process:

- Stage 1: **recognize** the problem

  Until you recognize that a **problem** exists, obviously you won't take any **action**. The **early recognition** of problems in your job is a skill that usually improves with experience. Experience will also tell you where something that might appear worrying can safely be ignored because it's unlikely to turn into a problem.

- Stage 2: accept **ownership** of the problem

  Not all problems that **affect** you are up to you personally to **solve**. If you do not have the authority or ability to solve a problem, it is usually wiser to pass it on to someone who does.

- Stage 3: **understand** the problem

  Once you know you have a problem and have accepted ownership of it, you must **define** it clearly, **find out** all you can about it, and **collect information** that will help you find ways of tackling it. In particular it pays to identify the causes of a problem.

- Stage 4: **choose** the best solution

  As will be emphasized in Session B, there are a number of useful approaches to **analysing** a problem that can lead you to a solution. In Session C we will concentrate on ways to generate new ideas when the problem cannot be solved using the known facts.

- Stage 5: **implement** the solution

  When you believe that you understand the problem, and can see a way of solving it, you can take action. Sometimes, caution is required because you cannot be sure that the plan will work. Sometimes you will have managed to find only a partial solution, and you will need to test this out before attempting to solve the rest of the problem.

- Stage 6: monitor and **evaluate** the solution

  After you've implemented a solution, you need to check whether it has worked, and whether it has had any effects that were not expected. Perhaps most important of all, you need to learn for next time.

The rest of this workbook looks at each stage in detail. Meanwhile, Activity 5 will get you thinking about the process as a whole.

Activity 5

Here is a flow-chart that illustrates the problem-solving process. Write in the actions that you think should appear in the six blank boxes on the right-hand side.

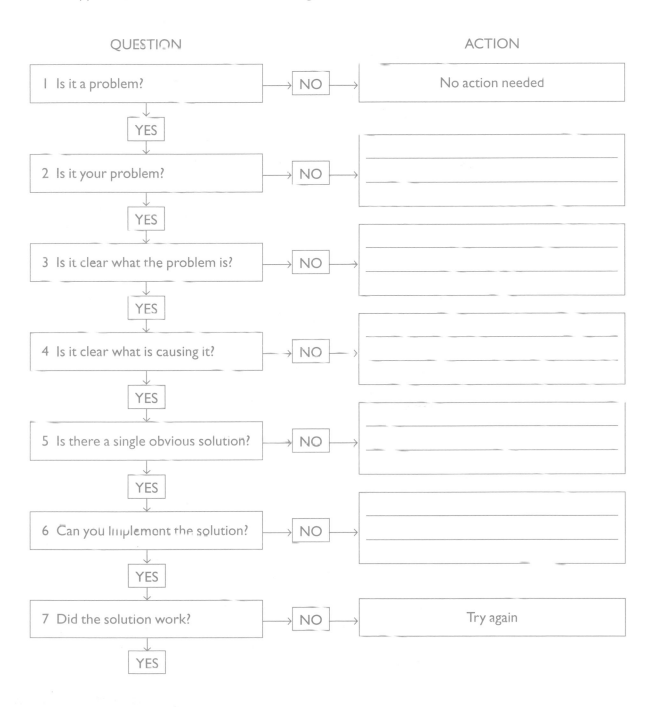

QUESTION   ACTION

1 Is it a problem? → NO → No action needed

YES

2 Is it your problem? → NO →

YES

3 Is it clear what the problem is? → NO →

YES

4 Is it clear what is causing it? → NO →

YES

5 Is there a single obvious solution? → NO →

YES

6 Can you implement the solution? → NO →

YES

7 Did the solution work? → NO → Try again

YES

You will find the answer to this Activity on page 97.

5 Stage 1: recognize the problem

Stage 1 starts with developing an awareness of possible problems before they hit you.

5.1 Looking out for problems

You may feel you have more than enough to do without looking for problems, but there are some advantages in asking yourself: 'What would happen if . . .?' or 'Supposing this were not to work . . .?'.

Activity 6 · 3 mins

Make a note of two advantages of actively looking out for potential problems.

_____

_____

_____

_____

You are often likely to find that you are trying to cope with more problems than you would like. This shouldn't, however, stop you from looking for more on the horizon. There are two reasons for this.

- The earlier you spot a potential problem, the better you'll be prepared to cope with it.
- When everything is going smoothly, there may be an opportunity to take a fresh look at things that you normally take for granted. You can then use problem-solving techniques to try to find a better way of doing them.

5.2 Is there really a problem?

On the other hand, it's a mistake to go too far in the other direction, and to imagine problems at every turn.

You may well have come across the kind of person who is always finding problems which aren't there. Often it's because of lack of experience, or fear of the unknown, or just a tendency to panic. Asking the question 'Are you sure?' can often save precious time and resources.

Are you sure there really is a problem?

Even when there really is a problem, it may not need a solution. Some problems solve themselves; others can safely be ignored.

Can you ignore it? Can you side-step it?

5.3 Is the problem worth solving?

Sometimes there is a real dilemma in trying to solve a problem, because we can see that its solution may result in further problems.

Desmond is a supervisor in a small family company. Although he enjoys his job very much, the company is not doing well. Desmond's problem is that he would like to earn more money. He goes to his boss and asks for a rise in salary. The boss says that the way that sales are going, this just isn't possible.

Desmond is pretty sure that he could get a job elsewhere for more money. However, he knows that if he does this, he will miss his present job, and the people he works with, very much.

Activity 6 ·

5 mins

If you were Desmond, what would you do?

_____

_____

_____

_____

_____

_____

There's no easy answer to this problem, and you may have felt you didn't have enough information. For example, it would help a great deal to know the reason why Desmond needs the extra money. Is it for some luxury, or is he really finding it hard to 'make ends meet'? Also, is Desmond taking other factors into account, such as his future career prospects?

Desmond's case is typical of the difficulties we all face in our lives. We would like neat problems with clear-cut answers, but our experience tells us that there is nearly always a price to be paid for solving a problem. For example, in medicine, tremendous advances have been made using drugs in the treatment of disease. Yet we are told that no successful drug has yet been discovered which does not have some adverse side-effect.

So it is often necessary to question the importance of finding a solution. It's worth asking yourself the following questions:

- Is there a solution to this problem?
- Will solving it be worth the effort?
- What price am I prepared to pay for solving it?

6 Stage 2: accept ownership of the problem

Once you've decided that:

- a problem exists;
- and needs solving;
- and is worth solving;

you then need to ask yourself: **Is the problem really mine?**

If it is, then you must accept ownership of the problem, and take responsibility for solving it. However, you may not get much benefit – or approval – from trying to solve problems that aren't really yours.

> Sometimes problems are SEPs – someone else's problem!

Selim was in charge of outpatients administration in a hospital. Patients often complained to him about the difficulty of parking their cars at the hospital. Selim sympathized, and he encouraged some of them to write to the hospital manager asking for the old tennis courts to be opened up for parking. In fact they sent a copy to the local newspaper, and there was some adverse publicity. The hospital manager was very annoyed to hear that Selim was behind all this, and reprimanded him. 'You are fully at liberty to report problems to me or anyone else,' she told him, 'but meddling in matters that don't concern you must stop.'

When you accept ownership of a problem, this implies that you will:

- take responsibility for solving it;
- put your personal energy and authority into doing so;
- ensure that those concerned know that you are accepting ownership.

Bear in mind, though, that even if you accept ownership of a problem, you are not necessarily on your own. Other people may be able to help you solve the problem, and indeed may have a **responsibility** to do so.

Activity 8 · 30 mins

**S/NVQs
CI.I, DI.I**

This activity is the first in a series of eight in which you will use a range of techniques to solve a problem that is currently facing you at work. They could jointly provide the basis of evidence for your S/NVQ portfolio. If you are intending to take this course of action, it might be better to write your answers on separate sheets of paper.

Select a problem that is currently facing you at work. It should be:

■ something important enough to justify spending some time on getting it right;
■ a problem which you 'own' and which you are responsible for solving;
■ difficult or complex enough for the solution not to be obvious from the start.

It could be:

■ a **deviation** problem, where something is not going to plan, and it's not clear why;
■ a **potential** problem, where something is starting to develop that may cause difficulties if it isn't dealt with;
■ an **improvement** problem, where there's a need to find better ways of doing things for the future (for example increased productivity, better safety, or changes to working methods).

Start by making a list of problems that might be suitable, marking them 'deviation', 'potential', or 'improvement'. Take time to think about them before you make your choice.

Now write down the problem you have selected and describe it briefly.

_____

_____

_____

_____

_____

EXTENSION I
Extension I is a checklist of all the main points covered in this workbook. You may find it helpful to refer to the checklist on page 92 whenever you identify and start to tackle a problem.

You will be asked to work on analysing and solving this problem at a number of points throughout this workbook, so make sure you have made a suitable choice. Remember that the problem should be **important enough**, and **difficult** or **complex enough**, to be worth working on. It should also be a problem that **you personally** are responsible for solving.

Self-assessment 1

10 mins

1 Rearrange these words to complete the definition below:

The definition of a problem is: **deal difficult is or resolve something to which with**.

_____

2 Here are the six stages of problem solving. Fill in the blank spaces using either the word **problem** or the word **solution**.

Stage 1: **recognize** the _____

Stage 2: accept **ownership** of the _____

Stage 3: **understand** the _____

Stage 4: **choose** the best _____

Stage 5: **implement** the _____

Stage 6: monitor and **evaluate** the _____

3 Define the three main types of problem:

a deviation problems

_____

_____

b potential problems

_____

_____

c improvement problems

_____

_____

The answers to these questions can be found on pages 94–5.

7 Summary

- It's a good idea to think about the problem before coming up with a solution.

- You are likely to encounter three main kinds of problem:

  - deviation problems, where something has gone wrong;
  - potential problems, ones that may be arising for the future;
  - improvement problems, where you try to find ways of improving performance.

- It is better to foresee and prevent problems than to wait till they have burst into the open. Most 'unforeseen' problems **could have been** anticipated.

- The six stages of problem-solving that are described in this workbook are:

  - Stage 1: **recognize** the problem;
  - Stage 2: accept **ownership** of the problem;
  - Stage 3: **understand** the problem;
  - Stage 4: **choose** the best solution;
  - Stage 5: **implement** the solution;
  - Stage 6: monitor and **evaluate** the solution.

- You should not waste time and energy trying to solve problems that are:

  - likely to go away of their own accord;
  - unimportant;
  - best dealt with by someone else.

- It's worth asking yourself:

  - Is there a solution to this problem?
  - Will solving it be worth the effort?
  - What price am I prepared to pay for solving it?

- When you accept ownership of a problem you are making a promise that you must be sure to keep.

Session B
Defining problems and causes

1 Introduction

Some problems are simple, and it's obvious from the outset what the solution will be.

> The college urgently needed a temporary clerical assistant to work in the admissions department. The choice fell on Dorene, but after only a week or so it was apparent that she was not capable of working to the right standard: she simply made too many errors.
>
> One solution could well have been to give Dorene extra training, but there was no time for this — admission applications were already pouring in. The college dismissed Dorene and took on a better-qualified person from an agency.

Dorene's temporary contract allowed her to be dismissed without notice, so there was no legal constraint on this solution. If there was a 'problem with the solution', it was perhaps the human factor: no one likes sacking people, or admitting that they have recruited the wrong person.

Not all problems are this clear-cut, however.

2 Stage 3: understand the problem

In this session we will deal with stage three of the problem-solving process – **understand the problem**. We will focus primarily on how to understand more complex problems by **defining** them and then **analysing** them in order to find the **possible causes**.

3 Define the problem

A problem must be clearly defined before you can expect to solve it. All problems, even simple ones, benefit from being clearly defined and stated, and a good test is:

Can you write it down?

Let's look at an example of a problem which initially lacks definition, and then see how much it helps to define it on paper.

> Bill supervises a team that repairs computer assemblies. He confides his problems to a friend over an after-work pint.
>
> 'The work just keeps piling up. I have to divide the team's time between repairing rejects sent over from Production and faulty items that are returned by customers. The boss is constantly telling me that this or that customer has complained about slow service, but he won't let us have any more staff. He just says I should get better organized. Production keep sending me more and more rejects, and they're always pressuring us too. Everyone's fed up, I'm fed up, and it's getting harder and harder to face it all.'

Activity 9 · 7 mins

Briefly define Bill's problem, as he sees it. Try not to make too many assumptions, and don't suggest solutions at this stage.

_____

_____

_____

_____

One way of defining Bill's problem is like this:

■ Bill's team does not seem able to cope with its workload. This is resulting in low staff morale, unhappy customers, and an unhappy boss.

> We will return to this case study – which we'll call **Bill's problem** – repeatedly during the remainder of this workbook.

This definition is helpful, but we can improve on it by defining the problem in terms of the **desired outcome**. In practice, this might have more than one side to it.

■ What does Bill want to achieve?
■ What does the company want to achieve?

Activity 10 · 10 mins

What would you say is the desired outcome to this problem:

a from Bill's point of view?

_____

_____

_____

b from the company's point of view?

_____

_____

_____

If we had asked Bill this question, he might have given one of the following answers.

- 'I simply want my team to keep up with the workload. That way everyone will be happy.'

- 'I'd like to prove to my boss, and everyone else, that they need to change the whole way of working around here.'

- 'All I want is a quiet life.'

- 'I want to reduce the amount of work they throw at my team.'

The company, on the other hand, will be concerned with ensuring the best possible mix of efficiency, service quality and productivity.

So while Bill is focusing on 'Why is there too much work?', the company is probably thinking in terms of 'Why isn't Bill delivering the goods?'

These are two very different views of the situation, and they imply that the solution is open to question. Bill wants a reduced workload, but for the company that will not be an acceptable solution.

3.1 Stating the problem clearly

A good starting point is to draw up a 'problem statement'.

Activity 11

6 mins

Use the 'problem statement grid' (below) to identify the key issues in Bill's problem. Tick the right-hand column if you think you need more information before you can answer this question.

Key issues	Need more information
1 Describe the problem briefly:	
2 What effect is it having?	
3 Where is it?	
4 When was it first noticed?	
5 Is there anything special or distinctive about it?	

It is not possible to answer Questions 4 and 5 on the basis of the information we have so far. However, we will come back to these in a moment.

The rest of the questions are fairly easy to answer. The problem is that Bill and the repair team are finding it difficult to meet the competing demands of the factory and the customers. This is creating stress among the team and damaging morale. It is probably also damaging relations with the customers. **Note that this statement of the problem expresses it from both Bill's point of view and that of the company.**

The problem lies in the repair section. (We have no evidence that other parts of the company are overloaded.) However, this does not necessarily mean that the **cause(s) and solution** also lie in the repair section!

Activity 12

Are there any other questions that it might be useful to add to the 'problem statement'?

_____

_____

_____

_____

_____

_____

In this case I would add three questions, though these wouldn't apply to all problem statements.

How big is the problem? – You could rate it from, say, 1 to 10 for seriousness.

Who ought to be helping to find its cause and solution? In the example we're working through, I would say that Bill's boss and the production manager also ought to be helping, because they have a direct interest in the outcome.

We can show this in a diagram (a useful and quick technique):

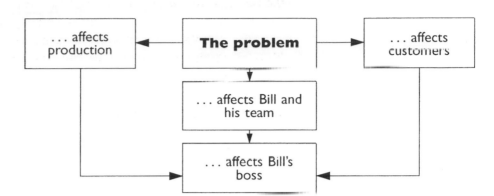

In the end all the pressure focuses on Bill's boss: Bill should be expecting a good deal of help from that direction!

What solutions have already been tried, and what was the outcome? Problems like this tend to drag on over a considerable time, and there may well have been some attempts to sort it out. Knowing what these were, and why they failed (as they presumably did) will save a lot of time when getting down to finding causes and solutions.

3.2 Spotting distinctive features

By identifying when a problem first appeared, and any unusual or distinctive features that it has, you can discover valuable clues about **causes**, which in turn will help find a **solution**.

> In a famous case study described by management experts Charles H. Kepner and Benjamin B. Tregoe, a company found that some of its extruded viscose elements were being contaminated with carbon. This was accurately timed as starting at 3.52 a.m. and ceasing at 4.03 a.m. There were four distinctive features about the problem:
>
> - It started and stopped abruptly.
> - There was no immediate recurrence of the problem.
> - Although four identical machines were operating at the time, only one was affected.
> - The machine had a total of 480 nozzles extruding filaments, and the problem affected all of them.

Sherlock Holmes would have been delighted to have such a wonderful set of clues!

Activity 13 · 15 mins

**S/NVQs
CI.I, DI.I**

This Activity is the second in a series of eight which could jointly provide the basis of evidence for your S/NVQ portfolio. If you are intending to take this course of action, it might be better to write your answers on separate sheets of paper.

Use the 'problem statement grid', with extra questions if appropriate, to help define the problem you identified in Activity 8.

Key issues	Need more information
1 Describe the problem briefly:	
2 What effect is it having?	
3 Where is it?	
4 When was it first noticed?	
5 Is there anything special or distinctive about it?	

Remember to be specific in completing the grid. If the problem suddenly began at 4.18 on a Friday afternoon, say so: this may point to the cause being something that happened immediately before 4.18.

3.3 Gathering information

To find the causes of a problem, you must gather information. (You must also gather information when generating possible solutions and establishing what the constraints – the restrictions – on the solution are. We will return to this subject in Session C.) Sometimes information will be available from the outset, but sometimes you will have to go looking for it. Information will allow you to define the problem precisely.

Activity 14

10 mins

What information have you been given about Bill's problem? List each point separately.

_____

_____

_____

_____

_____

_____

What else do you need to know?

_____

_____

_____

_____

_____

Sometimes, completing a problem analysis grid points clearly to the cause of the problem – but not often. The more important the problem is, the more it pays to take time to think.

4.1 Identify possible causes

Before we attempt a solution, we must identify the cause or causes of the problem. This means more Sherlock Holmes work.

Activity 16

More information is needed to establish the causes of Bill's problem. Where would you now concentrate your detective work?

_____

You need to concentrate on the point when the problem began – in January. Before January, there wasn't a problem. From January on, there was. Something must have changed. If we can establish what it was, we'll be a lot nearer a solution.

Activity 17

List some of the things that might have changed in January, and so have possibly given rise to a problem.

_____

_____

_____

_____

_____

Once you start thinking about this, you'll realize that a lot of things may have changed within one or more of the following:

- the work itself;
- the working environment;
- the product;
- management;
- the make-up of the team;
- physical factors.

Sometimes the thing that changed will be obvious (for example, if a highly experienced technician left the team in January and was replaced by someone who is incompetent). Sometimes there are many possibilities, none of them obvious.

The Kepner–Tregoe case study illustrates this point.

EXTENSION 2
The book in which Charles Kepner and Benjamin Tregoe explain how the 'carbon on the filaments' case was solved is a classic of management literature, now published under the title *The New Rational Manager*. See page 94.

> The analysis of the carbon-coated filaments problem clearly showed that something local and temporary had affected all the output nozzles on one specific machine. The investigators looked for sources of carbon. There were none in the factory, but outside there was a rail-yard, where coal-burning steam trains were used at all times of day and night. Could smoke have entered the air-intake of one machine but not the others? The answer proved to be yes. The four machines had separate intakes, many metres apart. It also transpired that on the night in question a steam shunting engine had been left for precisely 11 minutes in a position where its smoke drifted over just one of the four air intakes.
>
> Careful analysis had successfully traced the cause of the problem.

In the filament case, problem analysis showed clearly where the cause must lie. It was then a matter of logical deduction (plus a search for further relevant information) that led to the cause.

However, logical deduction is not always the best route to the cause, especially where the problem is less precise, and there may possibly be many causes.

Brainstorming is useful in two distinct parts of the problem-solving process – when you're looking for causes and when you're looking for solutions.

Often we need to do the opposite of focusing logically, and open up our minds to the widest range of possibilities, as in Bill's case. One technique for doing this is **brainstorming**.

4.2 Brainstorming

The idea of brainstorming is to come up with as complete a list of possibilities as you can, without worrying about whether they are brilliant or lousy, big or small. You can sort that out later.

Brainstorming is about **creativity**, and it's widely used in management for helping to solve problems and make decisions.

It is one of the many situations where two heads are better than one, and four or five are better still. The more different brains are at work, the bigger the storm of ideas.

How to brainstorm for causes of a problem

There are two stages in brainstorming. The first is creative, wide-ranging and should be free from analysis and judgements. Its rules are as follows.

- Everyone who is to take part gathers in a room away from the interruptions of normal work. Six to twelve people is the ideal number.
- A session lasts for a fixed time period: 30 minutes is about right.
- A chair or leader is chosen. His or her job is to define the problem, to remind everyone present of the rules of brainstorming, and generally keep control. Most important, he or she has to stop anyone trying to judge or evaluate the ideas put forward.
- Someone must note down all the ideas that are put forward. In a small group the leader could do this, by writing all ideas on a marker board or flipchart.
- Most important of all: everyone is free to put forward any idea at all, however bizarre or seemingly inappropriate. No one is allowed to say: 'That's no good' or 'I don't see the point of that' or 'That's just nonsense'.
- The idea of the session is to be creative, not logical.
- All ideas are evaluated **after** the session, not during it.
- Anyone who might have useful ideas can take part. It shouldn't be exclusive to 'management' or to people who are normally paid to think about the subject in hand.

When everyone is relaxed and ready, the leader asks for suggestions. Everyone should let their thoughts roam widely.

The leader jots down **everything** that **anyone** mentions that may have the slightest relevance to the issue. (It's best to write the suggestions on blank unlined paper, rather than try to make lists.)

- No suggestions should be omitted.

- No suggestion should be discussed or criticized.

The point is to amass the maximum number of suggestions, and more ideas than you'll eventually need, but you won't decide which to keep until later.

■ The suggestions should not be sorted into groups. This is for later too.

Stage two of brainstorming is completely different. It is a one-person job which is evaluative, critical, focused and logical. It consists of:

■ going through all the ideas that have been collected;
■ scrubbing out the daft ones;
■ sorting the others into groups;
■ highlighting the best of them.

Activity 18

Get together a group of colleagues (or your team) and try brainstorming the causes of Bill's problem – that is, the things that may have changed in January.

Jot down your ideas on a separate piece of paper. When you've finished, sort your ideas into groups.

Below is just one possible outcome of a brainstorming session on Bill's problem. The groups of causes selected are shown in the diagram (opposite). Your brainstorming session may well have come up with some different groups and lists of causes.

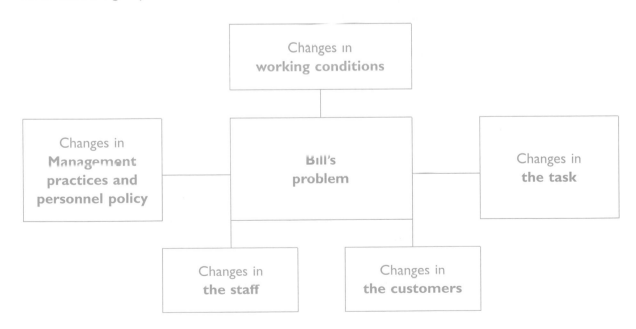

Brainstorming the possible causes of Bill's problem

All the suggestions have been grouped under the five headings, but the 'critical weeding' stage of the process has not yet begun.

Changes in the working conditions:

- relocation to smaller space;
- worse conditions;
- heating not adequate – hard to work;
- overcrowding;
- bad smells (ventilation problem);
- tools and equipment worn out, inadequate.

Changes in the task:

- increase in number of jobs to do;
- individual jobs harder to do;
- more processes, so longer to complete;
- new kinds of jobs – not so familiar;
- bigger proportion of faults – production problem;
- safety measures slowing down work.

Changes in the customers:

- getting more demanding;
- increased sales;
- different type of customers – don't know how to use product;
- change in distribution structure – more direct sales, so complaints coming back to us rather than to dealers?

Changes in the staff:

- experienced people have left – new ones not so quick;
- fall in morale for some other reason – Pay cuts? Fear of redundancy? Change of management? New working practices?
- Bill is new to the job – hasn't got leadership skills;
- jealousy over Bill's appointment.

Changes in management practice/personnel policy:

- boss not setting priorities properly;
- too much meddling;
- different priorities set;
- more paperwork to complete;
- safety measures slowing down work;
- Bill and/or team given additional tasks not mentioned?

Note that some causes, for example 'safety measures slowing down work', may appear in more than one group. On the other hand, some of the causes listed under some headings could be linked. Under 'Working conditions', 'relocation to smaller space' and 'overcrowding' are the same thing, while 'worse conditions' is a general term that could cover all of these.

4.3 Avoiding false assumptions

One of the commonest ways of taking the wrong path towards a solution is to make false assumptions. One of the benefits of brainstorming causes and solutions is that this is less likely to happen, because you are forced to consider all the options.

Activity 19

10 mins

Imagine you are concerned about the high turnover rate of staff in your department: too many are leaving and finding other jobs. You ask some of your staff what they think the problem is, and they suggest that a pay increase will help. As a result, you go to your boss and recommend a general pay increase.

What assumptions are you making? Why might some of these assumptions not be valid?

_____

_____

_____

After the exercise we have just carried out on Bill's problem, this should be clear to you. You are assuming:

- that you have discovered the cause (or at least a major cause) of the staff turnover problem (but what about work conditions, environment, motivation, and so on?);
- that increasing pay will reduce staff losses (but will it in the long term?);
- that the increased wage bill will not help to make your organization's products unprofitable or uncompetitive, so threatening everyone's jobs.

You may have thought of other assumptions.

When you're trying to analyse a problem, always ask yourself what assumptions you are making. Are your assumptions valid? Questioning your assumptions will help you find the right cause and consequently the right solution.

Using a problem analysis technique will help you identify false assumptions and pinpoint the problem more accurately.

4.4 Probing for the truth

When you're trying to understand a problem, it's always useful to keep asking questions.

To illustrate this, let's return to Bill's problem.

To quote Bill once again:

'The work just keeps piling up. I have to divide the team's time between repairing rejects sent over from Production and faulty items that are returned by customers. The boss is constantly telling me that this or that customer has complained about slow service, but he won't let us have any more staff. He just says I should get better organized. Production keep sending me more and more rejects, and they're always pressuring us too. Everyone's fed up, I'm fed up, and it's getting harder and harder to face it all.'

Asking 'why?' is something you will usually need to do in your own head, with a pencil and paper to help. You might perhaps imagine there are two voices speaking – one asking questions, and the other answering. Here's how it might go in Bill's case.

Why is the factory sending you more and more rejects?

Bill: I suppose they're increasing their output. I don't know for sure.

Is there another explanation? Is quality falling? Why don't you find out?

Bill: I could have a word with old Ted. Now I come to think of it, there's a rumour that they've been having trouble with parts suppliers. Perhaps Ted's in as much of a mess as I am.

Why is your boss so adamant about staffing levels?

Bill: Well, I agreed those staffing levels at the time of the budget, and he's a stickler for keeping to the figures. At budget time, though, we were running along smoothly.

Why are the two functions of factory repairs and customer repairs done within the same group?

Bill: A good question. In my last job we didn't do things that way. It means that I have to answer to two groups, effectively. Perhaps this is the crux of the problem. The system works well as long as we can cope with the workload. When we can't it means that I'm torn in two directions.

Would your boss listen to a well-presented argument for doing it differently?

And so on.

Activity 20

3 mins

What is the general outcome now? Do you think that after this mental discussion Bill would go back to his job in a more positive frame of mind?

_____

_____

There would be a very positive outcome from such an imaginary question-and-answer session. Now Bill has some ideas to think about, and he may be able to come up with some new approaches to his difficulties.

4.5 Fishbones: a way of analysing problems

Fishbone diagrams – also called cause-effect diagrams – are a simple visual technique for analysing problems where many possible causes may need to be considered. They can be drawn up from scratch, or built up from ideas developed by brainstorming.

The figure below is a fishbone diagram showing the five main groups of possible causes for 'Bill's problem'.

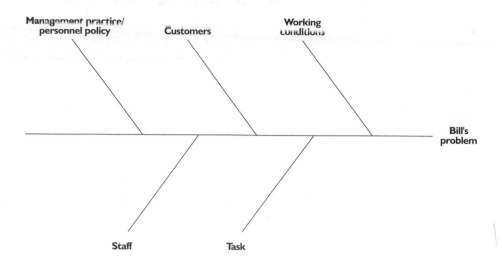

At the head of the fish is Bill's problem – unable to meet competing demands. Radiating from its spine are the five main groups of causes listed in the figure on page 29.

The next stage is to attach the more specific possible causes identified within each group (below).

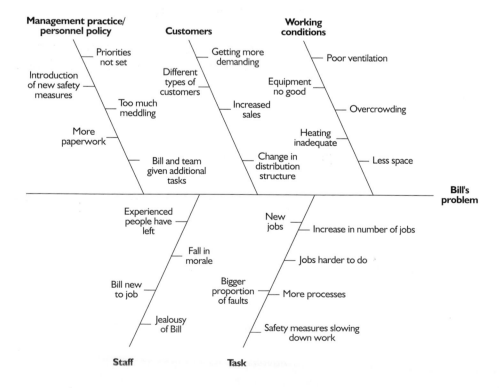

Once you have depicted all possible causes on a single sheet in this way, you can start to assess them individually.

The value of fishbone analysis is that:

■ it gives you a **complete picture** of all the possibilities;
■ it may enable you to discover that **more than one cause is involved**.

5 Other aids to understanding a problem

We have now looked at five practical techniques for defining a problem and seeking out its cause(s). They are:

■ describing the problem with a problem statement;
■ carrying out problem analysis;
■ brainstorming for possible causes;
■ asking why;
■ drawing fishbone diagrams.

There are a number of other approaches you can take to understanding a problem that will help you to identify both causes and solutions.

5.1 Technical aids

The first alternative approach we will consider is technical aids.

Activity 21

2 mins

Suppose you are in charge of a large office or workshop, and decide to redesign the layout, putting benches, tables, chairs, bookcases and cupboards in a more convenient arrangement. Would you:

a move the furniture around until it looked right ☐

b write down in words what you would like to achieve ☐

c use a computer layout program ☐

d make small to-scale outline cut-outs of each piece of furniture, and try them in different positions on an outline plan drawing of the work area, until you found the best arrangement? ☐

> Many tasks of this kind can be made a lot easier by computer software. These days cheap and simple programs are available for all kinds of 'problem' tasks, from journey planning to conducting appraisals to designing and planning gardens, homes and offices.

It's unlikely that you would want to keep moving the furniture around until you hit upon the right layout, so option (a) is not the answer. It always helps to state the problem and the desired outcome in words, so (b) would help, but it wouldn't be the complete answer. Options (c) or (d) seem by far the most sensible: this is a problem where it would help to see a diagram.

It is often useful to draw diagrams when defining problems. A picture is usually easier to understand than words. Good ideas, though, most often arise out of knowledge and experience. That's why it is important, when trying to solve problems, to call on existing knowledge: your own and that of others.

5.2 Drawing on your own experience

Experience – and learning – are of great help in problem solving. We often recognize, perhaps without even thinking about it, that a new problem is the same as, or similar to, one we've seen before.

Few problems are absolutely unique, and you will often find that you can apply general lessons that you've learned elsewhere.

> Lakshmi supervises a group of machinists in a clothing factory. Every few days the manager calls her into the office and gives her the specifications for ranges of garments that have to be put into production by a certain date. It's then up to Lakshmi to organize her team to complete the jobs on time.

Lakshmi is an active member of her local school's Parent-Teacher Association, and one day, out of the blue, she is asked to help organize the annual fête. At first, Lakshmi is very nervous about it, as she hasn't done the job before. She starts to write down some headings.

- What sort of fête do the PTA members want?
- Where will the fête be held?
- When will it be held?
- Who is available to help me?
- What can they do?

Lakshmi soon realizes that organizing the fete isn't really so different from organizing her team to make a new line of garments.

Activity 22

3 mins

How many 'points of similarity' can you find between organizing the fête and the organizing that Lakshmi normally has to do at work?

_____

_____

_____

_____

_____

The tasks appear to be quite similar in a number of ways.

- A specification has to be agreed ('what sort of fête?')
- Activities have to be planned to meet deadlines.
- People have to be organized.
- Information has to be communicated.
- Tasks have to be allocated.

There are also, however, some clear differences. For one thing, when she is at work, Lakshmi has authority to get things done. She is also very familiar with all the activities and processes involved. The fête isn't like that: she'll have to lead and motivate people who have no strong obligation to be helpful.

5.3 Drawing on other people's experience

Other people are a storehouse of knowledge and experience, and it makes sense to draw on these. Even if you've never come across a particular problem before, one of your colleagues almost certainly has.

> James was having trouble with Serena, one of his management trainees. Serena seemed intelligent and capable, but she was reluctant to take any instructions or advice from James. Instead, she went around boasting that all the work was easy, and that she'd be in a management post long before any of the others.
>
> James wasn't sure how to handle this, so he decided to talk to Paula, the training manager. What Paula had to say was helpful. 'We had a similar case about six years ago. I didn't try to argue with him. I just gave him a really difficult job to do, one that I knew everyone on the course would have trouble with, and left him entirely on his own to get on with it. When he got really bogged down he struggled for a while, and began to look more and more foolish. In the end he asked for my advice, and he showed more respect after that.'
>
> James decided to try the same technique with Serena.

Activity 23   20 mins

S/NVQ D1.1

This Activity is the fourth in a series of eight which could jointly provide the basis of evidence for your S/NVQ portfolio.

Make a list of the people who have more experience than you do – or experience that is different – and whom you might consult in relation to the problem that you are working on.

Use a separate sheet of paper, and list the names, a contact number or address, and the kind of help and advice they could give.

The obvious choices will be in your workplace, but don't restrict your choice to the people above you. Experienced team members can often help, and so can friends and former colleagues outside work.

Bear in mind that simply talking with someone about a problem can do a lot to help you get it clear in your mind.

If you go on to actually consult the people on your list, make a note of what you asked, what they said, what you did as a result and how it worked out. This could be useful evidence of your competence, and could be added to your S/NVQ portfolio.

5.4 Using rules and procedures

Rules, procedures, guidelines, manuals and handbooks are all designed to make problem-solving and decision-making easier by **telling you what to do** in a range of situations. In fact, it's useful to think of them as concentrated experience in written form.

> Computer buffs often say 'If all else fails, read the manual'.

It's amazing how often people ignore rules, instructions and guidelines, and get into difficulties as a result. You can probably think of instances of this yourself.

Activity 24 · 5 mins

Here are five problems to which the answer might lie in a rulebook, manual, set of guidelines, etc. Consider each problem from your own point of view, and write down which documents might provide you with help in finding a solution.

1 A team member has breached safety regulations, and you are not sure what disciplinary action is appropriate.

_____

_____

2 You need to replace some equipment, but the supplier you favour is not known to the organization. How can you establish whether the supplier is reliable?

_____

_____

3   Kelly wants to take some extra days of unpaid leave in addition to her annual holiday. Can you sanction this?

_____

_____

4   Some valuables have gone missing from a team member's desk overnight. What should you do?

_____

_____

5   A customer has written a long letter complaining about a member of your staff. How should you take this forward?

_____

_____

It's perfectly possible that some of these points are not covered by any rules, guidelines or handbooks in your particular organization. However, larger organizations will have all of them in writing somewhere. For example:

1   The health and safety handbook or the staff handbook will state what constitutes a disciplinary offence, and how it should be handled.

2   Where purchases can only be made from suppliers on an approved list, a procedure exists for suppliers to be added to it.

3   Rules about holiday entitlement, including how special requests are handled, will be in the staff handbook.

4   A security manual explains the procedure in cases of suspected theft.

5   This is perhaps the problem least likely to be covered by a written-down procedure. As a general rule such matters would be taken up by a suitably senior figure, possibly two levels above the person about whom the complaint was made.

There are also bound to be **people** who know the ins and outs of these policies and procedures.

Activity 25 · 20 mins

S/NVQ D1.1

This Activity is the fifth in a series of eight which could jointly provide the basis of evidence for your S/NVQ portfolio.

Consider the wide range of techniques for analysing the causes of a problem that have been discussed in this session.

■ Which of these techniques would you use to find the causes of the problem you are working on?

■ What are your reasons for choosing these particular techniques?

Note that using your chosen techniques to identify the causes of your problem could provide useful evidence of your competence which could be added to your S/NVQ portfolio.

This brings us to the end of an important session in which we have looked at defining and analysing a problem, and identifying the possible causes. If you have been working through a work-based problem of your own, you should now be able to say that you understand it. The next stage is to start looking for a solution.

Self-assessment 2

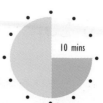

10 mins

1 There is a simple test of whether you can define a problem clearly. What is it?

_____

2 One item is missing from this list of questions that appear on a problem statement. What is it?

Describe the problem briefly:

What effect is it having?

Where is it?

_____

Is there anything special or distinctive about it?

3 These two techniques are very valuable when looking for the causes of problems. Decipher the anagrams to show what they are.

- SHINE FOB _____ analysis;

- SO BRING MARTIN _____

4 Here are three 'don'ts' to remember when brainstorming for causes or solutions. Fill in the blanks so that they make sense.

Don't omit any _____.

Don't _____ or _____ any suggestions.

Don't try to _____ the suggestions into _____.

5 What does a fishbone analysis give you?

_____

6 Complete the words below to explain why rules, procedures, manuals and handbooks can help you solve a problem:

Because they are:

c_____ e_____ in w_____ f_____.

Answers to these questions can be found on page 95.

6 Summary

- When problems are difficult or complex, they need to be defined with care, preferably with the help of a **problem statement**.

- You may need to define the problem from more than one viewpoint.

- It's useful to identify **distinctive features** about a problem: these may give a strong clue to the cause(s).

- You will need to **collect information** to find the causes of problems and possible solutions.

- If possible, draw up a **problem analysis** showing what the problem is, and what it could be, but is not.

- **Brainstorming** is a valuable tool for helping to solve problems. There are two stages:

  - the first wide-ranging, uncritical and creative;
  - the second critical and focused.

- When thinking about a problem, try to avoid making **unwarranted assumptions**.

- Probe into the truth by continually asking questions.

- Use whatever **assistance** you can get to help you find the causes of a problem, including:

  - technical aids such as computer software, diagrams
  - your own and other people's experience
  - manuals, rules, procedures, guidelines, handbooks, etc.

Session C
Finding a solution

1 Introduction

Very experienced people can often see a solution to a problem almost instantly; very **inexperienced** people also tend to go for 'instant solutions', though these often turn out to be the wrong ones. It is important to bear in mind that, until you are very experienced, it can pay to **delay** selecting a solution until you have thoroughly understood the problem.

In Session A we looked at the problem itself – what exactly is it? It is extremely easy to misunderstand problems, or to express them too vaguely, or to see them from only one point of view.

In Session B we went on to think about causes and considered some techniques for identifying what they might be. In this session we have to match solutions to causes – which is not always as easy as it might seem. This is all about Stage 4 in the problem-solving process: **choosing a solution.**

2 Stage 4: choose a solution

Before we go on to this, here is some information you have perhaps been curious about – the cause of Bill's problem. In fact, analysis of the causes came to the following conclusions.

- Working conditions had not changed significantly, and were not considered to be a cause.
- **The task had changed**: introduction of a new product range had led to quality problems, with an increased proportion of 'bugs' being discovered.
- The customers had changed, in that they were becoming more demanding, but this was considered to be a general change in the market about which nothing could be done.
- The people (Bill and the team) had not changed significantly, so the cause did not lie in this area.
- **Management practices had changed**: under the pressure of customer complaints and production problems, Bill's line manager was intervening too much and failing to set clear priorities.

3 What is a solution?

This may seem a strange question: a solution is whatever solves the problem, you may say.

Actually, this is unrealistic, as the following three examples illustrate.

3.1 When a solution is not a solution

Gerry and Kate hadn't bought a TV licence. Two reminders came, which they ignored. One day they saw a detector van down the street. Problem! They ran upstairs and pretended no-one was in. They ignored the loud knock on the door. Two hours later they saw the detector van drive away.

Activity 26

1 min

Was their problem solved? Explain your answer.

_____

_____

_____

_____

Super-Utility Management plc ran a 'one-stop shop' inquiry service and helpline for their two million customers. Over a hundred operators worked shifts in rather crowded premises in the city centre. Capacity was limited, and there were increasing delays in answering calls. Since call response times were a 'key performance indicator' for the industry, there was clearly a problem. Management decided that in order to expand and improve the service, they would have to relocate.

They chose new premises at a green-field site about ten miles from the city centre. There was plenty of space for expansion, but the relocation proved to be a fiasco from the staff's point of view. There were no local facilities such as shops and banks, so they had to make extra trips when they needed these things. Second, the in-house facilities that they had been promised (a rest room and a proper canteen) were cut back to save costs: there was just a corridor to sit in and a couple of vending machines. Finally, and worst, many staff found the site difficult to get to. Almost everyone could get to and from the old city centre site by public transport, even late at night. Now only about a fifth of them could use public transport. Others had to rely on taxis, and several were forced to buy cars for the first time.

There was a sharp fall in morale, and recruitment became difficult. Performance, instead of rising, fell.

Activity 27 · ☼ 1 min

Was the relocation a solution to the problem? Explain your answer.

_____

_____

_____

_____

Paula and James (see page 38) decided that the management trainee Serena was indeed an arrogant individual who would never fit in. They agreed that she would have to go. Paula didn't want to be seen to have picked 'a wrong 'un', so she and Bob decided to make Serena's life so difficult that she would resign.

Activity 28 · ☼ 1 min

Was this a solution to the problem? Explain your answer.

_____

_____

_____

_____

All three of these case studies featured 'solutions' that were not really solutions at all, though for different reasons.

■ In the first case, hiding until the detector van has gone does not solve the problem. Sooner or later the detector van will return, and next time Greg and Kate may not be so lucky.

Postponing a problem doesn't solve it – though it may give you time to work out a solution.

- In the second case, the company's 'solution' to deteriorating performance only succeeded in making the problem worse.

  A bad solution can make old problems worse and create unexpected new ones.

- In the last case, a solution that might well work should be rejected on moral, legal or policy grounds. Paula's proposal – essentially to drive Serena out of the company by treating her unfairly – would certainly be over-ruled by senior management. Note that Paula's reasons for selecting this option were dubious in themselves – she didn't want to have to sack Serena because this might reflect badly on her.

  Some solutions are unacceptable.

3.2 Constraints on a solution

Solutions to problems are always subject to constraints – limitations on what you can do. For example, as we have just seen, there may be **moral, legal** and **policy** constraints on what solutions can be adopted.

Activity 29 · 5 mins

Think carefully about this question. What other constraints might affect your choice of a solution to any of the problems you presently have to deal with? Jot down at least three.

_____

_____

_____

_____

The most obvious constraint is **financial**. Everyone has to work within budgets, and funds are always limited. The next obvious constraint is a **human** one: a solution may require skills that you and your colleagues do not possess. Then there is a question of **authority**: you may see a solution but not have the power to implement it. **Time** is also a consideration. Urgent problems call for quick solutions. Options that take too long are not acceptable.

Physical constraints can also be significant. A work overload problem can perhaps be solved by employing more people, but if there isn't the space to accommodate them, it isn't an option.

Finally – and you may not have thought of this – there may be **cultural** constraints. A solution may be lawful, moral, cheap, timely, physically possible and within your power to implement, but it's still ruled out.

Here's an example of a cultural constraint in operation.

For a fortnight the weather had been sweltering. Both staff and customers in the shop were complaining. When the temperature became unbearable, the manager told the staff they could wear T-shirts instead of the uniforms specified in the dress code.

The district manager reprimanded the manager on two grounds: first for allowing the dress code to be broken (this was a policy constraint); and second for making the decision without consulting him. The latter was not laid down in any rules or regulations; but the organization's culture was such that no manager was allowed to make a significant decision without referring it upwards first.

Cultural	Lack of authority	Time
Policy	**CONSTRAINTS ON A SOLUTION**	Financial
Moral	Legal	Physical	Human

3.3 What a solution must be

The first part of this session can be summed up like this.
A solution to a problem must be:

- **effective**: It must 'cure' the problem either permanently or for a reasonable period of time;

- **efficient**: It must solve the problem without creating lots of extra ones;

- **viable**: It must take account of the various constraints that apply.

Activity 30 · 2 mins

If there are only one or two constraints on a solution, you don't necessarily have to abandon it.

Suppose you have a solution that works well in every respect, other than the time it will take to be effective. Perhaps the time constraint is negotiable – that is, when all concerned have had a chance to consider its other merits, they will be prepared to allow it longer to work.

Which of the other constraints would you think are, at least in some cases, negotiable?

Financial	Yes	No
Human	Yes	No
Physical	Yes	No
Legal	Yes	No
Moral	Yes	No
Policy	Yes	No
Cultural	Yes	No
Authority	Yes	No

My personal experience suggests that all of these constraints may be negotiable, except for the legal and moral ones. As with the time constraint, when the solution is basically a good one, you may be able to make a case for more money and human and physical resources.

If you can rally wider support for your solution, you may also be able to overcome policy and cultural constraints, and influence is often an effective substitute for authority.

4 Identify possible solutions

For some problems there is only one solution. For others there may be many possibilities. It makes sense to assemble all the possible solutions before you make your choice. The one that works best may not be the first one that springs to mind, as another look at Bill's problem will illustrate.

In the light of what we now know about its causes, Bill's problem can be restated as follows.

> There is an increase in the number of faulty products which Bill and his team do not have the capacity to handle; this has resulted in stress and demoralization, which are exacerbated by management pressure.

There are three interlocking 'dimensions' here:

- too much work;
- lack of capacity;
- management pressure.

Together, these determine the nature **and the size** of the problem. We can actually show this problem as a three-dimensional shape – a cube, to be precise.

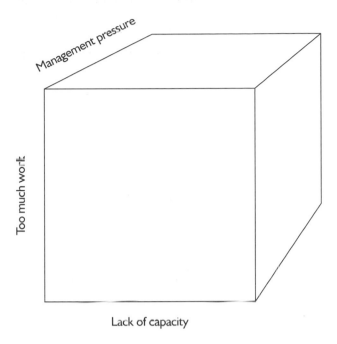

If the size of any of the three dimensions of the cube can be reduced, the overall size of the problem will be reduced.

Reduce them enough, and the problem disappears!

Activity 31

5 mins

Given the way Bill's problem has been restated and shown as in the figure above, what solutions can you suggest?

_____

_____

_____

_____

_____

_____

Logically, anything that reduces the size of one of the cube's three dimensions will help produce a solution. However, there is a difference between the three causal dimensions that we have identified. **Too much work** and **lack of capacity** are the main factors determining the size of the problem; **management pressure** simply makes it worse. So, while dealing with the management issue will ease the problem, it will not solve it. A solution to Bill's problem has to concentrate on:

- either reducing the number of faults sent for repair;
- or increasing the capacity to repair them.

4.1 Two contrasting approaches

Finding possible solutions is much like finding possible causes. There are basically two different strategies:

- the logical, focused approach;
- the broadly-based, creative approach.

The logical approach

The logical, focused approach is based on the information you have gathered about the problem and the cause(s). Within reason, the more information you have, the better.

You then study the information and make rational deductions about the solution.

Thus in the case of Bill's problem, the solution is clearly one of workload/ capacity rather than, say, of Bill's leadership or competence. The problem is not of Bill's making.

Looking at the two main dimensions of the problem, we can say with perfect logic that:

- reducing the number of faulty items being produced will solve the problem;

- increasing the capacity of Bill's team (by offering more overtime work, or employing more people) will solve the problem.

Activity 32 · 5 mins

We don't know much about the implications of adopting these solutions, but we can be sure that cost is a major consideration.

What comments would you make about the two logical suggestions for a solution?

a reducing faults

_____

_____

_____

b increasing capacity

_____

_____

_____

The mention of costs provided you with a strong hint. The company needs to make a profit; if its costs go up, profits will be under pressure. We already know that Bill's manager had ruled out increasing the staff budget, presumably for this reason. Reducing fault levels in Production is easily said but hard to achieve. It may involve operatives working more slowly, more inspection, better equipment, changed methods, etc. All of these also boil down to cost in the end. While making lots of faulty items must reduce profits, the steps needed to reduce the faults may – at least in the short term – be even more costly.

In practice, there may be many constraints against adopting a seemingly logical solution. We will come back to this issue shortly.

EXTENSION 3
If you are interested in developing your creative skills you might like to take up this extension, or one of the many other writings by 'lateral thinking' expert Edward de Bono. See page 94.

The creative approach

The other option in seeking a solution is to get away from narrow logic and approach the problem from different angles, using 'creative thinking'. This is another situation where a bit of brainstorming may work wonders. If you decide not to use a formal brainstorming session, it is still worth re-examining the problem from different angles.

In Session B Bill's problem was defined from both his point of view and that of the company. However, up to now we've focused on **internal** events that affect the company and its employees – repairs requested by Production aren't being done quickly enough, Bill's team is overworked, Bill is demoralized – and so on. These are certainly problems, but they are surely not the main concerns for a commercial company.

From a commercial standpoint the main problem is that **customers are complaining**. This presents a major risk to the company: a poor reputation for quality is easy to get, commercially damaging and exceptionally difficult to reverse.

The priority for a solution, seen from this angle, is not to make Production, or Bill, or Bill's team happy, but to make the customers happy.

So here are some suggestions. See what you think.

- There is obviously a quality control problem in Production. Sorting this out will solve the problem cleanly and completely, but it's easier said than done. It may take too long, be too costly, and require resources that don't exist in the company.
- Why not change the priorities? Why not have Bill's team deal solely with faults reported by customers, and provide an excellent service in this commercially sensitive area?
- Faulty items sent for repair by Production could be set aside until there's time to deal with them – or they could be thrown away.
- Perhaps the solution is to increase Production and live with the fault rate.
- Perhaps a new team within Production could be set up to deal with minor faults there.

Logical reasoning, which is deductive and focused in the Sherlock Holmes tradition, is often referred to as **convergent thinking**. Creative, wide-ranging approaches of the brainstorming type are the opposite: **divergent thinking.**

In general, the best long-term solution would be one that reduced the fault rates in Production, since this ought to be an objective for the company anyway. This would reduce customer complaints, and the workload problem would evaporate.

In the short term, the company might prefer a solution that ensured that faults reported by customers were dealt with promptly. This would give time to tackle the production quality issue.

Activity 33 · 20 mins

S/NVQ A1.3

This Activity is the sixth in a series of eight which could jointly provide the basis of evidence for your S/NVQ portfolio.

You should now be in a position to start generating possible solutions to the problem you first described in Activity 8. Take some time to do this now. If you have time, try to approach the problem from both the **logical** and the **creative** direction. Using more than one technique will give you different and perhaps contrasting angles on the matter.

Note down your possible solutions, describing them in sufficient detail for you to be able to evaluate them later.

Any work that you do on identifying possible solutions could provide useful evidence of your competence and could be added to your S/NVQ portfolio.

Perhaps you already had some ideas about the possible solution before you began Activity 33. However, when the problem is an important one, it is always worth taking time to examine possible solutions in a systematic way, as we have been doing in this Session.

5 Some solutions are better than others

You will no doubt find that there is often more than one possible – and acceptable – solution to many of the problems that you will encounter. How will you choose between them?

One approach is to use the effectiveness/efficiency/viability checklist on each solution and see which comes out best.

Another approach – and in many ways a better one – is to test the solutions against a set of objectives. These need to be rather more detailed than the 'desired outcome' referred to in Sessions A and B. Objectives are the **specific results** that you wish to achieve in solving the problem.

Of course, there are generally two or three objectives (known as **go/no go objectives**) that you **must** achieve in order to be able to say that you have solved the problem. But there may be others that it would be **desirable**, or perhaps just **nice**, to achieve at the same time.

You can in fact think in terms of three levels of objective:

- **must** objectives. If you don't achieve these, you don't have a solution.

- **want** objectives. These are things that it's valuable but not essential to achieve;

- **would like** objectives. It would be nice to achieve these, but it doesn't matter that much if you don't.

Rhoda has a problem with one of her staff whose work is erratic and who is not always reliable. Her overall 'desired outcome' is either to ensure that this person works to the right standard in future, or to put in motion procedures for replacing him.

Rhoda has worked out three possible solutions – A, B and C. She has then checked them against five specific objectives. If the solution delivers the objective, she gives it a tick.

Objectives		A	B	C
1	**Must** show offender how he can improve his performance	✓	✓	
2	**Must** ensure offender understands what will happen if no improvement	✓	✓	✓
3	**Want** to demonstrate to boss that I am a competent manager		✓	
4	**Want** to demonstrate to team that I can handle such issues fairly	✓	✓	✓
5	**Would like** to teach this person a lesson!	✓		✓
6	**Would like** to have the problem sorted out by mid-July	✓		

Activity 34

Look at Rhoda's checklist above. Which solution is best?

The best solution is: _____

You will find the answer to this Activity on page 97

5.1 Weighted objectives

There is a more sophisticated way of comparing how different solutions perform in terms of non-essential objectives. Instead of dividing these objectives rigidly into 'wants' and 'would likes', you give each such objective a numerical value, or 'weighting'.

'Weighting' simply means giving a bigger number to things that you value highly, and a smaller number to less important matters. In Rhoda's case the weighting of the four non-essential objectives on her list might look like this.

Non-essential objectives		*Weight*	*A*	*B*	*C*
3	Demonstrate to boss that I am a competent manager	5		✓	
4	Demonstrate to team that I can handle such issues fairly	10	✓	✓	✓
5	Teach this person a lesson!	2	✓		✓
6	Have the problem sorted out by mid-July	4	✓		
Scores	max	21	16	15	12

This method gives a different result: solution A wins by a whisker! Of course, it all depends on what weighting you decide to give each objective. (Remember that solution C is still ruled out because it doesn't deliver both the 'must' objectives.)

Activity 35 · 20 mins

S/NVQ A1.3

This Activity is the seventh in a series of eight which could jointly provide the basis of evidence for your S/NVQ portfolio.

Draw up your detailed objectives for the problem that you are working on for your assignment. If there are several non-essential objectives, lay them out on the lines shown on page 59.

Now evaluate the potential solutions that you developed in Activity 33 against your objectives.

When you have done this, give your best two or three solutions a further evaluation using the checklist below.

Rate the first two items from 0 to 5.

How effective is it?	0	1	2	3	4	5
How efficient is it?	0	1	2	3	4	5

Is it viable in terms of the following constraints:

Time	Yes	No
Financial	Yes	No
Human	Yes	No
Physical	Yes	No
Legal	Yes	No
Moral	Yes	No
Policy	Yes	No
Cultural	Yes	No
Authority	Yes	No

Where you have identified a constraint, you may find it useful to spell out what this means in practice. The fact that there is a constraint does not necessarily mean that your solution is not viable. You may be able to negotiate your way through it. This is particularly true of financial, human, policy and cultural constraints.

5.2 The final check

When you have identified a small number of solutions – preferably just one or two – that appear to be:

- effective;
- efficient;
- viable;

and seem likely to achieve your desired outcomes and specific objectives, there are a few final checks to make.

Ask yourself:

- How easy will it be to implement this solution?

  If you have two good solutions to choose from, the one that is easiest to implement should be your choice.

- What risks are attached to it?

  If you have two good solutions to choose from and one looks less risky than the other, then the one involving less risk should be your choice.

Activity 36   3 mins

Here are some pairs of 'risk factors' that might apply to any potential solution to a work-based problem, including the one you have been working on in this workbook.

For each pair, say whether (a) or (b) is the more risky, and why.

1 a This solution involves installing brand-new state-of-the-art equipment with which we are not familiar.

   b This solution involves installing extra units of familiar equipment.

   Which is riskier? _____

   Why? _____

   _____

2 a The manager has succeeded in working out a solution by himself, without involving his boss or the workteam.

   b Many colleagues have been involved in reaching a decision.

   Which is riskier? _____

   Why? _____

   _____

3 a There is plenty of time to implement the solution.

   b Split-second timing is needed to get the solution on stream in time for it to work.

   Which is riskier? _____

   Why? _____

   _____

4 a This is an ingenious but very complex solution.

   b This is a simple and rather obvious solution.

   Which is riskier? _____

   Why? _____

   _____

5 a We are confident that staff and customers will react favourably to this solution.

   b We are confident about the solution but don't have a clear idea of how staff and customers will react to it.

   Which is riskier? _____

   Why? _____

   _____

Do you agree that the riskier solutions are (a), (a), (b), (a) and (b) respectively? It should be fairly obvious why, though managers often make obvious mistakes! Whatever the brilliance and attractiveness of a solution, it is always relatively risky:

- to bank on new and untried ideas, equipment or people (1);
- for an individual to work out a solution without consulting and involving others (2);
- to have to work to tight time-scales (3);
- to adopt a complex solution (4);
- to proceed without evaluating the impact of a solution on the people it will affect (5).

The risk is of course that the solution will either fail or create unacceptable knock-on problems.

Before you go on to implement a solution, make sure you have a clear understanding of what the risks are. That way, you will have a reasonable chance of being able to minimize them.

Self-assessment 3

10 mins

1 Postponing a problem won't usually solve it, but it may have one advantage. What is it?

_____

_____

2 There are many constraints that may apply to a solution, but most are to some extent negotiable. Two generally are not. What are they?

_____ constraints

_____ constraints

3 A solution to a problem must be three things, which are spelled out in this block of letters. What are they?

A   B   C   C   E   E

E   E   E   E   F   F

F   F   I   I   I   I

L   N   T   T   V   V

_____

_____

_____

4 What is 'divergent thinking'?

_____

_____

5 Give an example of a 'creative thinking' technique.

_____

_____

6 At what stage should you evaluate the risks attached to a particular solution?

a When you have identified the cause(s) of a problem.

b When you have set your specific objectives.

c When you have gathered a number of possible solutions but before you select the best one or two options.

d After you have selected the best one or two options but before you make your final choice.

Answers to these questions can be found on pages 95–6.

5 Summary

- Some 'solutions' are not solutions at all.

  - Postponing a solution doesn't solve it.
  - A bad solution can make matters worse.
  - Some solutions are unacceptable.

- A solution that works must be:

  - **effective**: it will 'cure' the problem either permanently or for a reasonable period of time;
  - **efficient**: it solves the problem without creating lots of extra ones;
  - **viable**: it takes account of the various constraints that apply.

- Possible solutions to a problem can be found by logical deduction or by creative methods such as brainstorming.

- The best solutions can be selected by testing them against objectives, which can be thought of in terms of three levels:

  - **Must** objectives: if you don't achieve these, you don't have a solution;
  - **Want** objectives: these are things that it's valuable but not essential to achieve;
  - **Would like** objectives: it would be nice to achieve these, but it doesn't matter that much if you don't.

- Non-essential objectives ('musts' and 'would likes') can be weighted to give a more accurate indication of their importance.

- The final choice of a solution may be made on the basis of which is easiest and least risky to implement.

Session D
Implementing and evaluating a solution

1 Introduction

Sherlock Holmes was interested in solving problems, but once he had deduced who or what was responsible for the crime, his interest rapidly faded.

He took no part in the tedious business of assembling witnesses, taking statements, bringing the suspect to trial, reaching a verdict, determining a sentence and carrying it out.

In fact you may have noticed that most police and crime dramas also skip this part. In many cases, the villain disappears from the scene in a dramatic manner and there's no need for a trial at all.

However, real life isn't like detective fiction. When you've solved your problem you have to face up to implementing your solution. If you fail at this vital stage, all the effort that went before is wasted.

This session will take you through the two final stages of the problem-solving process: stage five: **implement the solution** and stage six: **monitor and evaluate the solution**.

2 Stage 5: implement the solution

You have by far the best chance of solving a problem when you have:

- thoroughly understood it;
- accurately defined and stated it;
- correctly identified the causes;
- set specific objectives;
- considered the effectiveness, efficiency and viability of your proposed solution(s);
- planned its implementation with care.

But you can still never be completely confident that the solution will work until you have implemented it.

The first point – an obvious one – is that you may need to get other people's **consent** before you can implement a solution. You may need to explain, convince, negotiate.

You may also need their **help** in implementing it. They may control resources, facilities and people without which it can't be done.

You will certainly need to **communicate** with a whole range of other people so that they understand what is happening. **In effect, you need to create an action plan.**

> Bill and his manager came up with an effective, efficient and viable solution to Bill's problem that was handled in two stages.
>
> First, new and clear priorities were set.
>
> - Faults reported by customers would be dealt with immediately; Bill was given a small extra budget for overtime to ensure that all such repairs could be carried out within 48 hours.
> - Faults reported by Production would in future have to wait until there was time to deal with them; no overtime was allowed for this purpose.
>
> Second, on a longer time-scale, the quality problem in Production was to be tackled. It was estimated that it would take up to three months to rectify it.

Activity 37

5 mins

Apart from Bill's own workteam, who would need to be told about what was going to happen?

_____

_____

_____

What other actions would Bill have to take to implement this solution?

_____

_____

As illustrated in the diagram below many people will need to be told in the first stage. This will mainly be the responsibility of Bill's manager. He or she will need the approval of higher management for the solution. Production will have to understand the need to give customers priority. Sales and marketing will need to know that service to customers is going to be improved, and they will need to pass this on to customers. Personnel will need to know about the new arrangements for overtime.

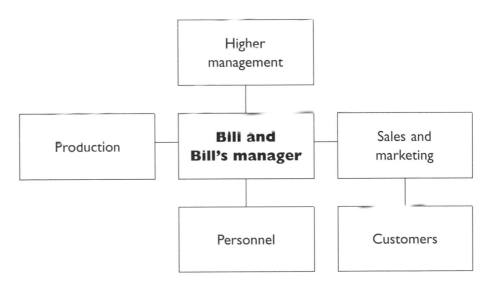

In order to ensure that the new priorities work, Bill will have to establish new systems. He will have to ensure that faulty items returned by customers are repaired within 48 hours. He must therefore log them in and record when they are sent out again. He will need to monitor progress daily, and allocate overtime immediately if it looks as though the standard won't be met. He must arrange a separate recording system for repairing production faults, and these items must be stored separately.

The second stage of the solution, tackling the quality problem in Production, will be even more complex, and we won't go into that here. (If you want to know more about quality issues, you might like to study another workbook in this series, *Understanding Quality*.)

With so many things to do to put the solution into effect, an action plan will be needed, which states:

- what is to be done;
- start date;
- who is to carry out the action;
- how they are to do it;
- resources required;
- target completion date.

(You will find further details in the Work-based assignment on how to draw up an action plan for implementing a solution.)

2.1 Managing risks and the 'downside'

This is also the stage where you need to think about any risks that you identified towards the end of Session C.

When drawing up an action plan, you should make a note of the risks and the action that you need to take to counter them.

3 Stage 6: monitoring and evaluation

Once a problem has been solved, there is a tendency to dismiss it from our minds. Our working life is full of problems, and no sooner do we finish with one problem than we're immersed in the next.

But, as with so many processes, the last stage – in this case monitoring and evaluation – is one of the most important if we are to learn lessons for the future.

3.1 Monitoring progress

It is rarely a good idea to implement a solution and then assume that things will run smoothly without any intervention on our part, especially where big changes are being made to a system or procedure. It is vital to monitor progress for some time after the changes are put into effect and then to evaluate its effectiveness.

Monitoring is the process of checking to find out how well the chosen solution is working. This can be done formally, for example through customer satisfaction questionnaires and computer printouts, or informally, by checking with the people involved to see if their problem has been resolved. You might even try out the improved system for yourself. Situations should be monitored at least until it becomes clear whether or not the solution is effective.

3.2 Evaluation

Evaluation is the process of comparing the actual outcome of the implemented solution (as measured by the monitoring) with your planned outcome, i.e. how successful the solution has turned out to be.

By evaluating your solution as it works in practice, you will achieve three important things:

- You will know whether or not it is working.
- You will see where and how it could be improved.
- You will learn something about how to solve your next problem better, quicker and more efficiently.

Activity 38

2 mins

How do you normally judge how well you have solved a problem?

_____

_____

Answering vaguely with something like 'by seeing whether it works' isn't really enough.

There are **four** approaches that you could use.

The first and most obvious one is to go back to the **objectives** that you set for the solution, and ask:

■ How well did it meet my objectives?

The second approach is to refer to **standards**. Many **deviation** problems (where something has gone wrong and needs to be corrected) are standard-based. For example, in the solution to Bill's problem it was decided to adopt a standard of repairing faulty items returned by customers within 48 hours. This is a clear standard, and if it is met, the solution is working, at least to that extent. (As you will realize, a standard may itself form part of an objective.) Thus, you might also ask yourself:

■ Are the required standards being met?

Thirdly, we could judge success in **quantitative** terms – for example, by comparing accident rates before and after implementing a safety improvement.

Activity 39

3 mins

Think of a problem that you've encountered where the effects of a solution can easily be measured in quantitative terms.

_____

_____

You may have suggested a number of things, such as:

- a problem of increasing productivity (you can compare the numbers produced before and after);
- a problem of wanting to earn more money (you'll be able to say how much more, if anything, was earned after your solution is implemented than was earned before);
- a problem of increasing sales (if the solution is a good one, sales will increase by a measurable amount, compared with what they were before).

All these are **improvement** problems. With most improvement problems it is possible to measure and compare solutions in some definite way.

Activity 40   3 mins

Now try to think of a problem where it is more difficult to measure the effects of a solution.

_____

_____

There are plenty of these. Some which come to mind are:

- the problem of trying to improve relations with your boss, or between members of your workteam;
- the problem of having to deal with a change of job;
- the problem of rearranging your office or workshop.

With all these kinds of problem, you may be able to say **whether or not** your solution was successful, but you would find it much harder to say **how well** you've succeeded in solving the problem. This is true of many **potential** problems.

The fourth approach is to look broadly at the 'pros and cons' – the **benefits and drawbacks**. Assuming that a solution has achieved roughly what was intended, you should focus on the downside – the 'cons'. What unwanted side-effects have there been, if any? How many people have been upset, how many orders lost, what additional problems created, what extra costs incurred?

Sometimes the result of applying a solution can have unexpected and unwanted effects. This happens usually when a problem has been defined too narrowly, or insufficient information has been gathered, or the solution has not been thought through in enough detail. The following story is a case in point.

Mike Royce was the supervisor of a DIY and builders' merchants outlet for a firm of timber merchants. In his team were two check-out staff, and five sales staff who dealt with the customers. Mike was overworked, and felt he needed an assistant. He therefore decided to ask Mukesh, a young salesman who seemed the most capable, to help him. He thought he'd better not inform the others about this arrangement, in case anyone got upset.

Mukesh was given a number of tasks, including looking after sales returns, which meant he had to get figures from each of the other sales staff. Within a couple of days, Mike was surprised to find that Mukesh had gone sick, and two of the older sales staff had threatened to walk out.

Activity 41

3 mins

Can you think of a possible reason for this unexpected result?

_____

_____

_____

_____

The reason was that Mukesh had been given no authority to do the job, and his appointment was 'unofficial'. The other sales staff had to learn from Mukesh himself what the new arrangement was, and two of the older ones had got upset about it. They wouldn't co-operate with Mukesh and Mukesh felt he just couldn't cope.

The result would not perhaps have been so unexpected to Mike if he had thought through what he planned to do.

Before applying a solution you need to check that you have thought it through. Once you have applied it, you need to work out its 'downside' – the unwanted effects – and perhaps draw up a balance sheet like the one shown below relating to Bill's problem.

Solution: *prioritize repair of faults reported by customers*	
Benefits	Costs/drawbacks
Customer service improved to standard Workload brought to acceptable level	Overtime spending greater than hoped Not able to make any significant impact on backlog of production faults Production manager annoyed that his faults aren't being repaired
Overall result: *positive*	

To sum up, evaluating a solution depends on how well you:

- have identified and defined the problem;
- are able to assess and measure the situation before a solution is applied;
- can define attainable and measurable standards;
- can assess the benefits and drawbacks flowing from the solution.

Implementing a solution can be the hardest stage of all. This isn't the time to 'shut your eyes and hope for the best', though. You will need to apply as much thought and care in putting your plan into effect as you did in developing it.

4 Looking back

Every time you go through the problem-solving process you have the opportunity to learn something that will help you do even better next time.

Let's go through some of the key points to think about when you look back on a problem.

- What caused the problem in the first place? Could it have been avoided?
- Have you taken steps to make sure that the problem won't recur?
- Was your initial approach to the problem the right one? What can be learned from the mistakes made in the early stages?
- Were you objective in your approach to the problem?
- What about the eventual price you had to pay for solving the problem: was it worth it, or would you have been better off not tackling the problem at all?
- Did your definition of the problem turn out to be correct, or were you forced to revise your perception of it?
- Did you have enough information to make a sound decision? Could you have got more?
- Are you confident that you will be able to recognize a problem of the same type in the future, so that you can use a similar solution?
- Can you use the result or method again, for a similar problem?
- Did you use all the help you could get? Were you surprised to find out who the most helpful people were?
- Could you have arrived at the result differently? Does it all now seem obvious?
- Would you tackle a problem like this in the same way again?
- What have you learned?

Activity 42

30 mins

S/NVQ A1.3

This Activity is the last in a series of eight which could jointly provide the basis of evidence for your S/NVQ portfolio. Whether you can complete it will depend on the exact nature of the problem you have been working on and how quickly and easily your chosen solution can be implemented and evaluated.

When you have had the opportunity to implement your preferred solution, evaluate it against the factors listed in the checklist opposite. The evaluation of how you went about solving your problem could provide useful evidence for your S/NVQ portfolio.

If your evaluation indicates that your solution was a mistaken one, it may not be too late to reverse your decision. If it suggests ways in which the implementation could be improved, you should of course take steps to do this.

In this workbook the examination of problem solving has taken you through six stages:

Stage 1: **recognize** the problem
Stage 2: accept **ownership** of the problem
Stage 3: **understand** the problem
Stage 4: **choose** the best solution
Stage 5: **implement** the solution
Stage 6: **monitor** and **evaluate** the solution.

Self-assessment 4

10 mins

1 Suppose a supervisor boasted to you: 'I had a problem of increasing the output of my workteam. I solved it: we are now doing 5 per cent more than last year!'

What would your reaction be? Would you:

a simply congratulate the supervisor for doing a first-class job ☐

b ask what the target had been for increasing output ☐

c ask what other supervisors in the same place of work had achieved by way of increased output? ☐

Briefly explain your choice.

_____

_____

2 Name three ways of evaluating the success of a solution.

_____

_____

_____

3 Which of the following are quantitative measures of success?

a Before the changeover, our performance was poor; now it is considered acceptable. ☐ Yes ☐ No

b The target was a productivity improvement of 3.5%. In the event we only achieved 1.75%. ☐ Yes ☐ No

c Our main objective was to ensure that Dave was able to operate the new machine to the correct safety standards. This was achieved. ☐ Yes ☐ No

d Average call duration had risen to 6 minutes 36 seconds. Following retraining it has fallen to 4 minutes 54 seconds. ☐ Yes ☐ No

e We are confident that the improved service for customer repairs will reverse the recent decline in sales. ☐ Yes ☐ No

Answers to these questions can be found on page 96.

5 Summary

- In most cases you will need the consent and **help** of other people to implement a solution to a problem.

- You will also need to **communicate** with various interested parties.

- Except in very simple cases, this implies that you will need to draw up an **action plan** showing who will do what, when and how.

- Once you have **Implemented** a solution, you should **evaluate** it. This will tell you three things:

  - whether or not it is working;
  - where and how it could be improved;
  - how to solve your next problem better, quicker and more efficiently.

- You can evaluate it in four ways:

  - by comparing the outcome with your original **objectives**;
  - by checking whether any specific **standards** are being met;
  - by making **quantitative** 'before and after' comparisons;
  - by drawing up a balance sheet of **benefits and drawbacks**.

- You should follow up your implementation in two other ways:

  - by **monitoring** the progress of the solution (things seldom go entirely smoothly);
  - by **looking back** over the experience to see what you can learn from it.

Question 7   During the brainstorming session, a couple of members of the team repeatedly make suggestions that the rest think are silly, and which aren't written down. What is going wrong?

Question 8   The experience of managers and other experts in an organization is often available in a concentrated form. Where can you find it?

Question 9   What can you gain by doing a fishbone analysis?

Question 10   In what sense might a solution be worse than the problem?

Question 11   A solution to a problem must be viable. What is meant by this?

Question 12   Deductive, focused, rational. What is being talked about here?

Question 13   What are the 'go/no go' criteria for a solution to a problem?

Question 14   List three factors that would tend to make a solution relatively more risky.

Question 15   What should an action plan for implementing a solution contain?

Answers to these questions can be found on pages 98–9.

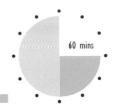

60 mins

2 Workbook assessment

In every organization there are established procedures and set ways of thinking that persist long after they have ceased to be useful. Managers, supervisors and team leaders often find themselves having to overcome such barriers in the course of dealing with what may be called **improvement problems**.

Let's examine a case in point.

> Bettina has recently been put in charge of the accounts office of a small chain of garages. She is expected to compile a range of data from the branches every week, and finds that many hours of her time are taken up with this. The branch managers are very busy and, although they are always prompt to send in car sales data, most of them have to be reminded time and again to send in the other reports. These include performance data on sales of parts and servicing, labour (hours worked), inquiries handled, discounts and miscellaneous costs.
>
> When Bettina has all the sheets, she has to enter them on the computer, and perform certain calculations. The individual and totalled figures are then passed on to the senior management team, who send a summary to the chairman.
>
> Being new to the job, it occurs to Bettina to ask 'why?'.
>
> - Why are the branch managers so reluctant to send in the data, apart from car sales figures?
> - Why must the figures be collected once a week? Why not once a month, for example?
> - Why does the management team need all this data?
> - Why does the chairman need them? What does he do with them?
>
> After asking a lot of questions, she finds out that:
>
> - Car sales figures are the over-riding priority, perhaps not surprisingly, since this is the main source of revenue for the group.
> - There is constant pressure on the branch managers to improve sales. However, branch managers never get any feedback on the

other data they have to submit. To them, it's just an irritating chore.

■ The management team do use these other data. Actually they enter summaries of Bettina's figures into their own computers. From these they compile four-weekly 'management reports', which are useful in various ways. They are not interested in reacting to these data on a weekly basis.

■ Once or twice a year, attention turns to these other 'performance measures', and branch managers are called together for a 'gee-up'. No-one takes this very seriously, though a manager whose branch performs badly may get a 'grilling'.

Suggest some changes to the system which would achieve the dual objectives of reducing Bettina's workload, while still ensuring that all concerned get the information they need.

3 Work-based assignment

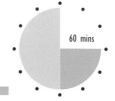

60 mins

S/NVQs
A1.3, D1.1,
D1.2

The time guide for this assignment gives you an approximate idea of how long it is likely to take you to draft and write up the plan. Your written response to this assignment may provide the basis of appropriate evidence for your S/NVQ portfolio.

What you have to do

Your assignment is to draw up an action plan for implementing the solution to the problem that you have been working on throughout this workbook.

You will need to spend some additional time discussing the issues with colleagues, checking details and thinking about the assignment. The result of your efforts should be presented on separate sheets of paper.

Before you start, look forward to the action plan for your personal development under Reflect and review on page 91. This action plan contains just four column headings:

■ Issues
■ Action
■ Resources
■ Target completion date.

What you should write

Action plans vary, depending on their purpose. The plan for implementing a solution to a problem will probably need to include column headings for:

- **action** (state briefly what is to be done);
- **start date**;
- **who is to carry out the action** (for example you, a team member or another colleague);
- **how they are to do it** (this is optional, because although you need to know how, it does not necessarily have to go on the plan);
- **resources required** (money, time, materials, equipment, vehicles, etc.);
- **target completion date**.

It is up to you to decide what column headings you need. You may decide you need extra ones, for example to show **who else is affected** by an action, and **who needs to be kept informed**.

Draw up your implementation action plan in six simple stages.

- **Stage 1** Draft the layout, showing the column headings you intend to use.

- **Stage 2** List all the principal actions needed. Include the communication aspects of the plan, such as announcing it to team and colleagues, and consultation with your line manager.

- **Stage 3** Re-arrange the actions in their logical order. For example, 'Brief staff on new priorities for repairing faulty units' would come before 'Inform customers of new standards for repairs', but after 'Agree solution with higher management'.

- **Stage 4** Decide how long each of the actions in the sequence is going to take (include preparation time – a staff briefing may only take a few minutes, but preparing it can take half a day).

  Bear in mind that two or more actions can often run in parallel, provided that neither depends on the other being completed first. This is a useful way of saving time.

- **Stage 5** Make a final version of the action plan layout. (It is a good idea to make some photocopies before you fill it in.) Fill in the details you have listed above, and add 'target completion' dates.

- **Stage 6** Discuss the final version with your team and colleagues, and modify it if necessary.

  - Does everyone understand what they have to do?
  - Does the timescale make sense?
  - Will the whole process be completed soon enough?

The assignment is to complete and submit a thorough and logical action plan. Of course, if you are dealing with a real problem, you should use your action plan to help you implement your solution. Any notes you add on how well the plan is working may form the basis of evidence for your S/NVQ portfolio.

Reflect and review

1 Reflect and review

This workbook has been all about how to deal with problems in a systematic way. It advises you:

- to hold back and think;
- to step back and analyse;
- to look back and learn.

This obviously isn't necessary for all problems, because sometimes a solution isn't needed, and at other times it's obvious what it must be. But the need for systematic problem-solving is undoubtedly real. As Perrin Stryker puts it in his introduction to Kepner and Tregoe's original version of *The New Rational Manager*:

> ... the cost of unsystematic and irrational thinking by managers is undeniably enormous. If he wants to, any good manager can easily recall from experience a wide assortment of bungled problems and erroneous decisions. As an executive of a large corporation long honoured for its good management once said to me, 'The number of undisclosed $10,000 mistakes made in this company every day makes me shudder.'

The whole point is that problem-solving and decision-making needn't be haphazard: these are skills that can be learnt. So let's review what **you** have learnt!

The first objective was:

■ When you have completed this workbook you will be better able to describe and analyse problems.

    ■ This is a matter of systematic thinking and using simple techniques. What new techniques have you learned? In what practical situations have you tried them out?

_____

_____

_____

_____

The next objective was:

■ When you have completed this workbook you will be better able to identify the cause or causes of problems.

It's amazing how often people look at a problem, and then go straight to proposing a solution without pausing to think about what the problem really is. One repeatedly hears things like 'Sandra's work was not up to scratch, so I gave her a written warning'. A little thought and investigation might have revealed that this was a purely temporary problem, or that there was a medical explanation, or that Sandra needed more training but didn't want to admit it, and so on. Knowing the cause can help us avoid taking actions that might be more damaging than the problem. It can often point us in the direction of a simple and low-cost solution.

    ■ Are you now both ready and able to look at the causes of a problem before jumping to conclusions about the solution? Describe briefly how you now go about this.

_____

_____

_____

_____

Quite a lot has been said about both logical and creative approaches to discovering causes of problems and to generating possible solutions. It has been recommended that you seek other peoples' advice, and also try to look at the problem from different angles. It is always necessary to challenge your own assumptions, and it is often necessary to challenge existing ideas and ways of doing things in the organization.

This brings us to the third objective:

■ When you have completed this workbook you will be better able to generate a range of possible solutions and decide which will work best

■ How would you now go about generating possible solutions? To what extent have you developed creative thinking skills, especially brainstorming?

_____

_____

_____

_____

Then we come to the last phases of the problem-solving process. Here there may be a difficulty. After putting lots of energy and brainpower into analysing problems, causes and solutions, you have to implement the best solution, monitor and evaluate it. This may seem the least interesting and rewarding part, but if the solution doesn't work, everything that went before has been a waste of time. A little more effort to ensure the solution is working, and to modify it a bit if necessary, will bring dividends. And last but not least, every problem-solving cycle is potentially a learning experience which can help make you a better manager.

Our final objective was:

■ When you have completed this workbook you will be better able to implement your chosen solution and evaluate its effectiveness.

■ Are you putting enough effort into implementation, monitoring and evaluation? What more could you do to make your solutions work even better?

_____

_____

_____

_____

2 Action plan

Use this plan to further develop for yourself a course of action you want to take. Make a note in column 1 of the issues or problems you want to tackle, and then decide what you intend to do, and make a note in column 2.

The resources you need might include time, materials, information or money. You may need to negotiate for some of them, but they could be something easily acquired, like half an hour of somebody's time, or a chapter of a book. Put whatever you need in column 3. No plan means anything without a timescale, so put a realistic target completion date in column 4.

Finally, describe the outcome you want to achieve as a result of this plan, whether it is for your own benefit or advancement, or a more efficient way of doing things.

Desired outcomes				
1 Issues	2 Action	3 Resources		4 Target completion
Actual outcomes				

3 Extensions

**Extension 1
Problem-solving
checklist**

Points from Session A: Problems large and small

■ Do you take time to think before 'solving' a problem?

■ Can you stand back from the problem and think about it in an objective way?

■ Is the problem a real one?

■ Can you ignore it? Is it someone else's problem?

■ Is the problem worth solving?

Points from Session B: Defining problems and causes

■ Can you write down a clear definition of your problem?

■ Can you express it in terms of the desired outcome?

■ Can you draw up a more detailed 'problem statement'?

■ Have you gathered enough information about the facts surrounding the problem?

■ Can you draw up a 'problem analysis'?

■ Are you sure you aren't working on false assumptions?

■ Have you brainstormed for possible causes?

■ Have you 'asked why' in order to probe deeper into causes?

■ Are you prepared to challenge accepted ideas?

■ Do you need to draw a fishbone diagram (cause-effect diagram) to help establish the cause?

■ If the cause isn't yet clear, are you able to use other resources to help discover it, such as:

   ■ computer software?
   ■ your own experience?
   ■ other people's experience?
   ■ rules and procedures?

- When studying a possible cause are you able to answer these questions:

  1 Does this cause really exist?
  2 Does it explain what the problem is, and what it is not?
  3 Is there anything about the problem that It doesn't explain?
  4 If this cause doesn't explain the whole of the problem, does it explain part of it?
  5 If this cause (or causes) had not arisen, would the problem have arisen anyway?

Points from Session C: Finding a solution

- Have you applied both logical and creative approaches to seeking possible solutions?

- Have you had a brainstorming session?

- Have you looked at the problem from a variety of angles?

- Will your solution(s) be effective (i.e. will they cure the problem either permanently or for a reasonable period of time)?

- Will your solution(s) be efficient (i.e. will they solve the problem without creating lots of extra ones)?

- Will they be viable in the light of the various constraints that apply?

- Have you assessed your solutions in the light of your desired outcomes?

- Have you worked out your specific objectives, and assessed your solutions against them?

- Have you considered the relative risks of your solutions?

- Have you thought about how to counter or minimize those risks?

Points from Session D: Implementing and evaluating a solution

- Have you worked out whose consent and help you need to implement your solution?

- Have you worked out who you need to communicate with about the solution?

- Have you created an action plan?

- Have you identified the risks and found ways to counter them?

- Have you decided what basis you will use for evaluating how well your solution works in practice?

- Have you drawn up a balance sheet of the benefits and the 'downside' (costs and other drawbacks) that the solution has produced?

- Have you been monitoring how the implementation is going?

- Have you looked back and learnt from the experience?

Extension 2

Book   *The New Rational Manager: An Updated Edition for a New World*
Authors   Charles H. Kepner and Benjamin B. Tregoe
Edition   2002
Publisher Kepner-Tregoe Inc.

This is an updated version of one of the best selling management books of all time. Based on the work of US management consultants Kepner-Tregoe Inc, the book describes in great detail the processes they have developed for solving problems, making decisions, anticipating future problems, and appraising situations. The book uses case studies (one of which is featured in this workbook) all of which illustrate that, no matter how mysterious the problem, they can usually be solved by careful analysis of information.

Extension 3

Book   *Lateral Thinking for Management*
Author   Edward de Bono
Edition   1990
Publisher Pelican Books (Penguin), London

The well-known author and broadcaster Edward de Bono has made a career from creative thinking. He has written a number of books which advocate the use of a technique he calls 'lateral thinking', as opposed to the application of logic, which he describes as 'vertical thinking'.

4 Answers to self-assessment questions

Self-assessment 1 on page 13

1 The definition should read:

The definition of a problem is: **something which is difficult to deal with or resolve.**

2 Here are the six stages of problem-solving correctly completed.

Stage 1: **recognize** the problem
Stage 2: accept **ownership** of the problem
Stage 3: **understand** the problem
Stage 4: **choose** the best solution
Stage 5: **implement** the solution
Stage 6: monitor and **evaluate** the solution

3   The three definitions should read as follows:

   a   deviation problems are where something has gone wrong, and corrective action is needed.

   b   potential problems are where problems may be arising for the future and preventive action is needed.

   c   improvement problems are about how to be more productive, efficient and responsive in the future.

Self-assessment 2 on page 42

1   The simple test of whether you can define a problem clearly is **whether you can write it down**.

2   The item missing from the list of questions that appear on a problem statement is shown below:

Describe the problem briefly:
What effect is it having?
Where is it?
When was it first noticed?
Is there anything special or distinctive about it?

3   When you decipher the anagrams you should get these two techniques:

- **fishbone** [SHINE FOB] analysis;
- **brainstorming** [SO BRING MARTIN]

4   The three 'don'ts' to remember when brainstorming are:

Don't omit any **suggestions**.
Don't **discuss** or **criticize** any suggestions.
Don't try to **sort** the suggestions into **groups**.

5   A fishbone analysis gives you **a complete picture of all the possible causes of a problem**.

6   Rules, procedures, manuals and handbooks can help you solve a problem because they are **concentrated experience in written form**.

Self-assessment 3 on pages 63–4

1   One advantage of postponing a problem may be that it **gives you more time to find a solution**.

2   The two constraints that are generally not negotiable are **moral** and **legal** constraints.

3   The three things a solution must be, and which you can make out of the block of 24 letters, are **effective**, **efficient** and **viable**.

4   Divergent thinking is a broad, outward-looking and creative approach to ideas.

5   Perhaps the most well-known example of creative (divergent) thinking is brainstorming. Another example is lateral thinking.

6   The correct answer is (d). You should evaluate the risks attached to a particular solution after you have selected the best one or two options but before you make your final choice.

Self-assessment 4 on page 78

1   If you simply wanted to be polite, you might choose (a). It would be interesting to know the answers to (b) and (c) though, wouldn't it? If, for example, you learned that all other supervisors had increased output by at least 10 per cent, you might not be so impressed by the boasting supervisor.

2   There are in fact four ways of evaluating the success of a solution to a problem:

■ comparing the outcome with your objectives;
■ measuring it against standards;
■ comparing 'before' and 'after' in quantitative terms;
■ drawing up a balance sheet of benefits and costs/drawbacks.

3   Statement (a) is **not** quantitative (it is **qualitative**); statements (b) and (d) **are** clearly quantitative, as they contain numbers. Statement (c) is **not** quantitative, but it is perfectly valid in spite of that. Statement (e) is no more than wishful thinking, and tells us nothing at all about whether the solution has succeeded, either in quantitative terms or otherwise.

5   Answers to activities

Activity 1 on page 1

Try the question on your friends: you'll probably be surprised at how many opt for the £1 million pounds, without a moment's thought.

In fact, option (b) would give you £10,737,418.23 after 30 days!

Unless you do sit down and work it out, though, it is only possible to guess at the answer to this question (unless, of course, you've seen it before). In fact, if option (b) was limited to, say, three weeks instead of a month, you would be far better off with option (a).

**Activity 5
on page 7**

The flowchart should look like this (don't worry if you haven't used quite the same words as those used here).

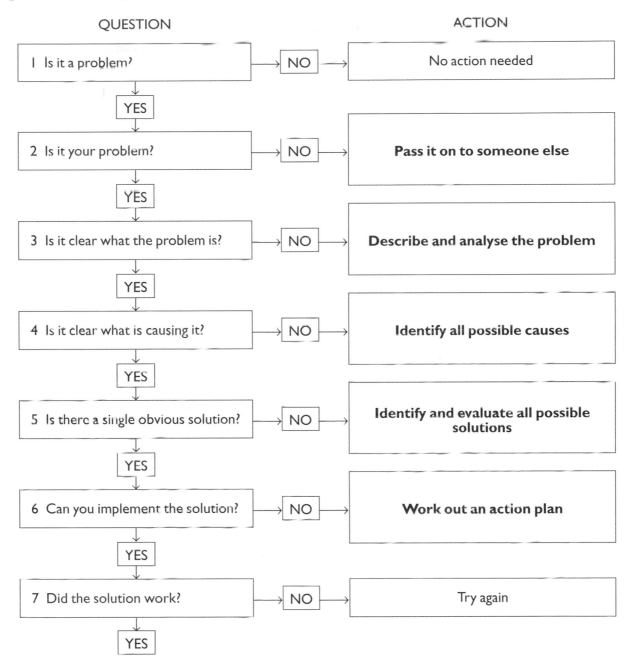

QUESTION

ACTION

1 Is it a problem?	→ NO →	No action needed
↓ YES		
2 Is it your problem?	→ NO →	**Pass it on to someone else**
↓ YES		
3 Is it clear what the problem is?	→ NO →	**Describe and analyse the problem**
↓ YES		
4 Is it clear what is causing it?	→ NO →	**Identify all possible causes**
↓ YES		
5 Is there a single obvious solution?	→ NO →	**Identify and evaluate all possible solutions**
↓ YES		
6 Can you implement the solution?	→ NO →	**Work out an action plan**
↓ YES		
7 Did the solution work?	→ NO →	Try again
↓ YES		

**Activity 34
on page 59**

The 'musts' are the minimum objectives. They are **'go/no go criteria'**: any solution that does not deliver them is 'no-go'. That rules out Option C, because it does not show the offender how he can improve his performance.

The choice is therefore between Options A and B, which both deliver the minimum objectives. The best choice appears to be B, because it also delivers **both** of the 'want' objectives, which are the next most important. Option A delivers one 'want', plus both the 'would like' objectives, but this still puts it below Option B in rank order.

6 Answers to the quick quiz

Answer 1   Before setting out to solve a problem you should **think about it**.

Answer 2   A problem is **something that is difficult to deal with or resolve**.

Answer 3   The three main types of problems are **deviation**, **potential** and **improvement** problems.

Answer 4   The first stage in the problem-solving process is to **recognize the problem**. The last is to **evaluate the solution**.

Answer 5   Writing down a problem helps you clarify the details in your mind, and sometimes even suggests a solution right away.

Answer 6   The pairs of statements in a problem analysis sheet tell you what the problem **is**, and what it **could be, but is not**.

Answer 7   In brainstorming, all suggestions should be noted down, and no-one should be made to feel that their ideas are silly.

Answer 8   The concentrated experience of managers and other experts is often to be found in the organization's guidelines, handbooks, manuals, etc.

Answer 9   A fishbone analysis should give you a complete visual picture of the possible causes of a problem.

Answer 10   A solution might be worse than the problem if it causes more or worse problems than there were to begin with.

Answer 11   A viable solution is one that works while also taking account of the various constraints that apply.

Answer 12   **Deductive, focused** and **rational** are words that describe the logical, as opposed to the creative, approach to finding possible causes of and solutions to a problem.

Answer 13   The 'go/no go' criteria are the objectives that a solution must deliver if it is to be considered a success.

Answer 14   Risk factors for a solution include:

- relying on new or untried ideas, equipment and people;
- failing to consult and involve others;
- tight timescales;
- complexity;
- failure to evaluate the impact that the solution will have on the people it affects.

Answer 15   An action plan for implementing a solution should contain details of what is to be done, when, how and by whom. It may also contain details of risks and what will be done to counter them,

7 Certificate

Completion of this certificate by an authorized person shows that you have worked through all the parts of this workbook and satisfactorily completed the assessments. The certificate provides a record of what you have done that may be used for exemptions or as evidence of prior learning against other nationally certificated qualifications.

Pergamon Flexible Learning and ILM are always keen to refine and improve their products. One of the key sources of information to help this process are people who have just used the product. If you have any information or views, good or bad, please pass these on.

INSTITUTE OF LEADERSHIP & MANAGEMENT

SUPERSERIES

Solving Problems

....

has satisfactorily completed this workbook

Name of signatory ....

Position ....

Signature ....

Date ....

Official stamp

Fourth Edition

INSTITUTE OF LEADERSHIP & MANAGEMENT
SUPERSERIES
FOURTH EDITION

To order – phone us direct for prices and availability details
(please quote ISBNs when ordering) on 01865 888190